LOCH LOMOND
& THE TROSSACHS

LOCH LOMOND
& THE TROSSACHS

INCLUDING THE ROB ROY COUNTRY

RENNIE MCOWAN

PEVENSEY GUIDES

*Page 1: Cottages on the old drovers'
road at Brig o' Turk
Pages 2–3: Reflections in Loch Dhu,
to the east of Ben Lomond
Right: A quiet path for strollers in the
Strathyre woods*

The Pevensey Press is an imprint of
David & Charles

Copyright:
Text © Rennie McOwan 2000
Photographs © Roy Rainford 2000 except
pp43, 45, 49, 63, 75, 80, 85, 87, 98 by the
author

First published 2000

Map on page 6 by Ethan Danielson

A catalogue record for this book is
available from the British Library.

ISBN 1 898630 09 7

Page layout by
Martin Harris Creative Media
Printed in Hong Kong by
Hong Kong Graphic
for David & Charles
Brunel House   Newton Abbot   Devon

CONTENTS

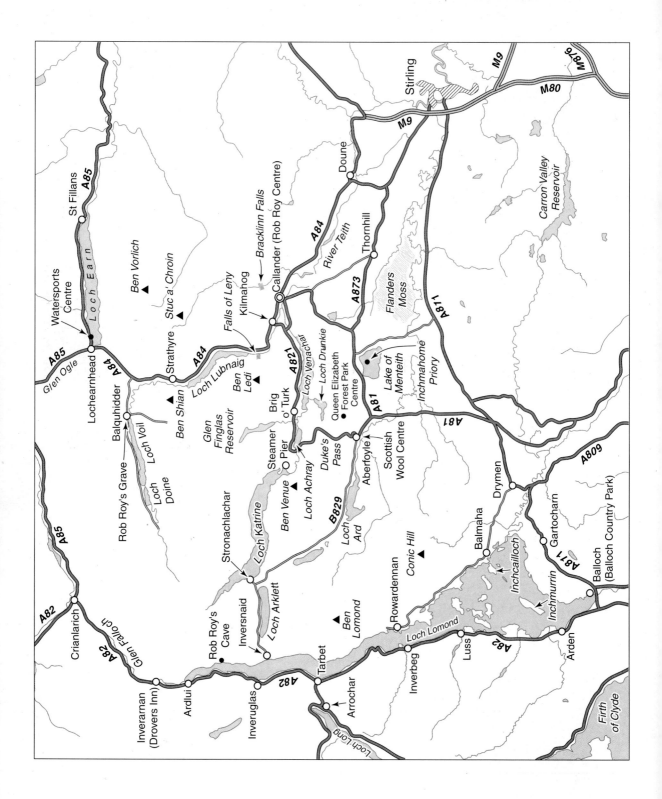

Kings and Shepherds, Warriors and Poets, War and Peace

FROM THE HIGH GROUND and castle mount of royal Stirling, the visitor sees a great blue wall of mountains to the north-west, the true boundary between Highland and Lowland. The Scottish writer Neil Munro said that in past times all roads stopped at Stirling and the far-off glens and straths only contained bridle paths and the routes taken by cattle drovers: here were two ages, one of paper, one of steel. This heaped-up skyline cradles, or is part of, Loch Lomond, the Trossachs and the Rob Roy country where the clans of old tended to hold their land by the sword and frequently infuriated monarchs and their advisers who had faith, some of the time, in legal documentation. It is a boundary, too, of different cultures and languages. Gaelic was the language of the southern and central Highlands, although it has virtually vanished in our own day, just commemorated in many place names. The people of the lower ground or in court circles in past centuries spoke Lowland Scots or court French.

Bluebells make an eye-dazzling display in the early summer, at the side of the Duke's Pass, in the Trossachs

A COLOURFUL PAST

THE LAND COVERED IN THIS BOOK once hid the fugitive King Robert the Bruce during the fourteenth-century Scottish Wars of Independence. It saw Queen Victoria open the Loch Katrine water scheme in the nineteenth century, which changed the health of the city of Glasgow. It knew the people of pre-history who put their forts on strategic knolls and their crannogs on the lochs. It has known charcoal burners and illicit whisky makers, foresters and poets, shepherds and quarrymen, ramblers and artists. The probing Romans sent patrols here, some never to return. It is a land where the Celtic nature lore of spirit life in trees and plants and tales of goblins and faeries, co-existed with Christianity. A fey book called *The Secret Commonwealth* was written in the seventeenth century by the Rev Robert Kirk, minister at Balquhidder and Aberfoyle, an account of the lifestyle of the faeries. Tradition has it that he is not really buried in the forestry village of Aberfoyle (although his grave can be seen), but so annoyed the faeries that they turned him into a pine tree; he can be 'seen' on the top of neighbouring Doon Hill to this day.

Modern roads now run where the eighteenth-century military engineers built roads in a bid to tame the clans. The great natural forests of the past have largely gone, replaced by extensive tracts of modern conifer forestry. However, new woods of oak and other deciduous trees are planned and this will make a definite link with the past because the Gaelic alphabet largely consists of the names of trees and plants, a sign that the people of old lived amid trees. The old name for Scotland, Caledonia, may take its name from the Gaelic for 'wooded stronghold'.

This territory became the homeland to various clans – Stewarts, Grahams, Fergussons, Buchanans, Colquhouns (pronounced 'calhoon'), MacLarens, MacFarlanes, Campbells, MacNabs, and the best known of all, Clan Alpin, the 'Children of the Mist', the persecuted but tenacious MacGregors. Their main hero, Rob Roy MacGregor, has been called the Scottish Robin Hood because he took from the rich and gave to the poor, but unlike Robin Hood he is entirely factual – modern research shows him to have been an able leader who saw off powerful enemies. Surprisingly, he died in his bed at Inverlochlarig Beag, in the Braes of Balquhidder, in 1734. Liam Neeson's 1995 film *Rob Roy*, and Walt Disney's 1953 version *Rob Roy, the Highland Rogue*, are not far from the truth, and there is a visitor centre named after Rob in the town of Callander, sited in the shadow of Ben Ledi and on the banks of the River Teith.

Cottages in the village of Luss on the west shore of Loch Lomond

Above: A beautiful show of wild roses at Luss

Opposite: Towering Ben Lomond overlooks the waters of Loch Ard, near Aberfoyle

Wild flowers carpet the banks of a burn at the Duke's Pass, in the Trossachs

This area of the southern Highlands gave the world a new word, 'blackmail'; it also helped inspire two of the world's best known pieces of music. The MacGregors and others said to Lowland lairds that if they paid protection money the MacGregors would not steal their cattle and would stop others misbehaving. The word 'black' comes from nefarious deeds and 'mail' or *mal* is an old Scots and Gaelic word for rent or payment. 'Borrowing' cattle in past times was regarded as more of a manly sport than a crime.

The writer Sir Walter Scott, one of the fathers of the historical novel and modern tourism, in 1810 wrote an epic poem of romance and war, *The Lady of the Lake*, set mainly in the Trossachs, that beautiful area around Loch Katrine and Loch Achray. (The word 'Trossachs', which may mean 'transverse glens' or, more appropriately, 'the bristly ground', is also used nowadays for a much wider area.) The poem was a runaway success and brought thousands of visitors to the area. Scott's verses include a section called 'Hail to the Chief', and this has been set to music as a march which is played when American presidents appear at functions. The composer Schubert also set some of Scott's verses to music: he read a religious stanza in the poem which includes the Latin words, Ave Maria ('Hail Mary' from St Luke's Gospel in the Bible), and this prompted Schubert to write his own, world-famous 'Ave Maria'.

Older folk recognise Callander as Tannochbrae in the black-and-white television serial *Dr Finlay's Casebook* (that locus has now moved to Auchtertmuchty in Fife). The popular series was based on a story by A.J. Cronin, one of many literati who came to this area and who also included Robert Louis Stevenson, the Wordsworths, Boswell and Johnson, Charles Dickens, James Hogg, Robert Burns, Nathaniel Hawthorne, Jules Verne and many others.

FLORA AND FAUNA

THIS IS AN AREA OF BEAUTIFUL MOUNTAINS: Ben Venue above Loch Katrine; Ben Ledi, where Beltane, the Celtic new year, was celebrated on its summit; the rocky peak of Ben A'n (originally Am Binnean, the Pinnacle), a favourite with rock climbers; the big peaks of Stuc a' Chroin and Ben

Vorlich above Loch Earn; and the heather-clad Menteith Hills which excite geologists because they are part of the Highland Boundary Fault which runs across Scotland from the Isle of Arran to the port-town of Stonehaven. There are miles of enriching walking and cycling, plus one woodland car drive, in the modern woods of the Queen Elizabeth Forest Park, near Aberfoyle, where Forest Enterprise has a visitor centre and there are many lochs, some large, some semi-hidden: Lubnaig and Venachar, near Callander; Arklet, sited between Loch Katrine and Loch Lomond; Achray, in the Trossachs; Earn, north of Strathyre, where there is an award-winning sports centre; Chon and Ard, both reached from Aberfoyle; and the Lake of Menteith, on the southern fringe of our area. Augustinian monks had a priory here, on Inchmahome ('inch' means an island), and Mary Queen of Scots, then a child, was taken there to prevent her falling into English hands; the Earls of Menteith are buried here, too.

Above all, there is Loch Lomond, internationally known because of the famous song about the 'bonnie banks', and massive Ben Lomond, the beacon mountain, looking down on wooded islands which contain the ruins of a convent and a burial ground, and bolt-holes for out-of-favour nobles and their families. The busy A82 runs up the west shore of the loch, past little villages like Luss, used as the site of Glen Darrach for the Scottish Television series *High Road*, and up past the old drovers' inn at Inverarnan. The wooded east shore is part of the long-distance footpath, the West Highland Way, which runs 95 miles (153km) from Milngavie (pronounced 'mul-guy'), near Glasgow, to Fort William. There are cross-loch ferries, much pleasure cruising, and bird and nature reserves.

Loch Lomond is shaped like a tadpole and cuts right through the Highland Boundary Fault; at 23 miles (39km) it is the biggest sheet of fresh water in mainland Britain, its top end being situated in the Highlands and its lower only half an hour's drive from Glasgow. It, too, has known strife. Norway once ruled parts of Scotland's west coast and the islands of Orkney and Shetland, and in the thirteenth century tried to coerce the youthful Alexander III – one of Scotland's best kings – into an unsatisfactory peace deal. But the king dragged out the negotiations and eventually the Norsemen were caught by storms and defeated. They dragged their longships from tidal Loch Long ('loch of the ships') across the two-mile (3km) Tarbert isthmus to Loch Lomond and sailed down the loch to sack the settlements of Lennox. Nowadays Loch Lomond is a favourite place for thousands of Scots and other visitors, both on land and water. There are visitor centres at Balmaha, on the east shore, and at Luss and Balloch Castle country park.

The famous song tells of a Scot executed at Carlisle, in the north of England, where a Jacobite garrison surrendered to the Duke of Cumberland's Hanoverian forces during the 1745 Jacobite Rising when the exiled Stuarts tried to regain the British throne. His lover will return by foot but he – his spirit or soul – will return by 'the high road'. Some folksong

From top to bottom: Mosses and lichen in Glen Finglas, in the Trossachs; sunlight defines the bluebells in the Achray Forest Drive; lichen adorns the rocks and the trees

11

historians dispute all this, but it is widely believed and constantly sung and deserves its moving place in the folklore of the mountains and the loch.

That very popular song, *The Wild Mountain Thyme*, comes from the Rob Roy country. It is based on a song/poem written by Robert Tannahill, a Paisley weaver, and was originally called *The Braes o' Balquhidder*. Another that is frequently sung is *Bonnie Strathyre*, the latter a place which was originally a rest halt for cattle and is now a forestry village between Callander and Lochearnhead; the hill overlooking the village was believed to have been a haunt of faeries.

This area of the red deer and the golden eagle is outstandingly beautiful and inevitably has the hand of people upon it, although not adversely so. There are hydro-electric dams and reservoirs, lines of pylons, modern roads and conifer forestry. The modern visitor can go cruising on Loch Katrine, once the MacGregors' heartland, can shop for woollens or specialist knitwear or souvenirs in Aberfoyle, Callander or Kilmahog, or stay or eat in a wide variety of hotels, restaurants, guest houses and other sites. Also, the story of the Loch Katrine water project is as absorbing as any of the clan battles and feuds.

This area is well served with roads: the main A84 from Callander links with Strathyre, Balquhidder and Loch Earn. The A821 breaks off north of Callander and links Brig o' Turk, once a royal hunting area and beloved of artists, with the Trossachs; a high section, the Duke's Pass – named after the landowner, the Duke of Montrose, and still the A821 – links with Aberfoyle where there is a Trossachs centre. The south-east corner of Loch Lomond

Above: Callander and District Pipe Band at the Rob Roy & Trossachs Visitor Centre, Callander

Left: A picturesque farm situated on the shore of Loch Earn

13

has minor roads – the B829 running to the little harbour of Inversnaid, and the B837 from Drymen to Balmaha and Rowardennan. The village of Gartocharn has a small mound hill nearby called Duncryne, just off the A811 from Stirling, which has very fine views of the Loch Lomond islands. But all land changes to some degree and new deciduous woods are planned for Glen Finglas, near Brig o' Turk, and also for the shores of Loch Katrine, for Loch Lomond-side, and for several places elsewhere. They will make the land look as it was in past times.

Ben Lomond and the surrounding ground is now in the care of the National Trust for Scotland; in December 1995, this area, along with adjacent Forestry Commission land, was designated as the Ben Lomond National Memorial Park, dedicated to all who gave their lives in the service of their country. It opened in November 1997. The whole area of the loch is currently looked after by the local authorities as the Loch Lomond Park. In September 1997, the government recommended that Loch Lomond and the Trossachs be Scotland's first National Park, and this has been approved by the Scottish Parliament. Other corners have special environmental protection.

Explore and enjoy, but with sensitivity, because we are all guardians of this beautiful area.

Above: Balmaha harbour, Loch Lomond

Opposite: Conic Hill, above Balmaha, gives magnificent and far-reaching views over the Loch Lomond islands

1 Mountain and flood: Callander and the Ben

THE TOWN OF CALLANDER is both a frontier site and a gateway to the Highlands. The traveller from the south sees a prominent mountain overlooking a landscape of hill farms, small woods and occasional pieces of rough moorland and there is a strong sense of moving into an area wilder than the flat fields of the low country. The colours, too, can be vibrant – big blue mountains, green fields and woods, the small grey town tucked away beneath high wooded bluffs, and burns and rivers rippling implacably on their seemingly endless way.

Callander town is a relatively new creation, although the old parish stretched as far as Loch Katrine. There would always have been some form of habitation here because the site dominates key passes which are like sword-cuts through the mountains. Long ago the name was spelled Kalentare, perhaps derived from the name of a burn; the earliest Celtic form is caleto-dubron, meaning hard water. The town's broad main streets and central square were laid out by the Crown Estate

Above: Sheep country – a Highland farm near Callander

Opposite: The Falls of Leny, north of Callander

Fishing in the River Teith is an exhilarating, yet peaceful sport

Commissioners who took over the forfeited Clan Drummond lands after the failure of the 1745 Jacobite Rising. A little later some other houses were constructed for pensioner-soldiers returning from the Seven Years War (1756–63) which was fought in Europe, North America and India between Prussia (with British financial support) and a coalition of Austria, Russia and France. Among other things, it left Britain as the world's chief colonial power. Callander nowadays is a residential and tourism town of about 2,000 people, with many shops, pleasant walking and a golf course where scores are high because the players are distracted by the views.

When the land had a harsher, more wooded and marshy look, the Romans came here. The legacy they have left in the town is a site alleged to be a camp, marked by the well known Roman Camp Hotel and mounds by the River Teith which were reputed to be Roman forts. In fact, the real Roman fort, a marching camp, lies outside the town at Bochastle, at the crossroads of the A84 – which runs northwards through the Pass of Leny to the forestry village of Strathyre, to the entrance to Balquhidder glen and the water sports centre of Lochearnhead – and the A821 which runs past Loch Venachar and Brig o' Turk village to the Trossachs proper. On a small knoll known as Dunmore, above where these modern roads now run, the Caledonian tribes had a fort, and it is easy to think of warriors from both sides confronting one another. A prominent boulder lies close to the fort, left by a glacier and called an erratic by geologists, although it is known locally as Samson's Putting Stone – legend has it that a Celtic giant threw it there.

Kilmahog nowadays is a handful of houses, two large shops on the site of a mill specialising in Scottish knitwear and souvenirs, a hotel, and an old church and kirkyard which gives that corner its name: 'kil' meaning an ecclesiastical site, the rest a corruption of a Celtic saint's name, often given as Chug. The powerful Livingstones – Earls of Callander – held sway here and a castle once stood on the banks of the River Teith. James V1 of Scotland (1st of England) entrusted his young daughter Elizabeth to their care, and she was later to become the Winter Queen of Bohemia. It was through her that the Hanoverians inherited the throne of Britain – she provides the crucial link between the Stuart kings and the House of

Hanover. In fact, the reign of her husband, Frederick, was less than a year – hence the tag given to him by his enemies, that when spring arrived he would melt away like the winter snows.

There are really two Callanders: the big houses that lie on the higher ground close to the wooded cliffs known as the Crags, and the generally smaller ones on the flatter ground reaching down to the River Teith. The long main street has a scattering of shops, hotels and guest houses, and in modern times a kind of Callander promenade has developed whereby visitors walk up one side of the street, cross over and go down the other. The centre is dominated by Ancaster Square, named after a family which has long links with Callander, and here there are two links with the past: the memorial to the dead of two world wars, the figure of a clansman upon it, a link with the martial past; and the old church of St Kessog, the patron saint of the area. The latter has now been converted into the Rob Roy and Trossachs visitor centre, where the life of that great Highland hero is presented for modern audiences. The steps of the church and the square are often the site of Highland dancing, and this is often where pipe bands perform – and the echoing of the pipes when heard from the high ground above the town can really pull back the centuries. A tip for visitors: never speak of the '*skirl* of the pipes' (although people do) because it makes real pipers wince: a 'skirl' is a false note.

The riverside area is known as The Meadows, and children congregate here to play and feed the ducks. It marks the confluence of two rivers: the Leny, which comes through the twisting, wooded pass of that name and emanates from Loch Lubnaig and the Eas Gobhain from Loch Venachar, which becomes the River Teith. In summer this is a popular corner for strolling, but in winter, after prolonged rain or melting snow, the two rivers can become angry and the flat, grassy parkland can sometimes be under water – in bad years it can swirl up to the main street and invade some of the houses and shops. Here, too, is Tom an Cheasaig, the mound of St Kessog (or Kessaig) alongside an old graveyard and the striking red sandstone bridge. This is an evocative corner. The bridge was built in 1908, but looks very much older. At the far end of The Meadows the old railway line has been turned into a cycle and walkway which runs to Strathyre and Balquhidder. The graveyard in this corner includes a memorial to the renowned eighteenth-century Gaelic evangelist, Dougal Buchanan, who is buried there; another memorial to him can be found in Strathyre village. Gaelic has gone and churchgoing has declined, but he was once revered all over the Highlands.

Some people and families leave a mark on an area, and one is certainly Sir Walter Scott. He spent holidays with the Buchanan family at Cambusmore House, to the south of Callander, and made expeditions from there to research *The Lady of the Lake*. A second is Lord Esher, secretary to Edward VII and George V, a noted book collector and friend of J.M. Barrie (who gave us 'Peter Pan'); his home is now the Roman Camp Hotel, and he

Bright tartans on display at Kilmahog Woollen Mill

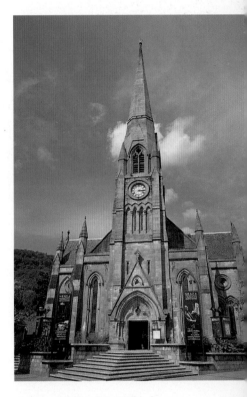

A converted church in Callander now houses the Rob Roy and Trossachs visitor centre

also built a now ruinous mausoleum near Loch Lubnaig. The third is the Clan MacNab: look high up on the walls of the Dreadnought Hotel and a man's head can be seen. 'Dread Nought' is the MacNabs' motto. The MacNabs, who were very powerful, had a spat with the MacNeishes and reduced them to little more than a robber band. Then the MacNeishes robbed a MacNab pony train at Christmas and this was a last straw for the MacNabs. Their chief had remarried and his wife, sensitive about the courage of her sons, is reputed to have uttered the words which became a Highland proverb: 'Tonight's the night, if the lads are the lads.' The MacNabs carried a boat over the hills from Loch Tay to Loch Earn, rowed up the loch in darkness, surprised the MacNeishes on their tiny island, a former crannog which can be seen near modern St. Fillans, and wiped them out. They cut off the head of the MacNeishes' chief, hence the stone memorial at the hotel which was built by a modern MacNab.

BEN LEDI: 'THE BEN'

The majestic Ben Ledi overlooks Callander and the River Teith

BEN LEDI IS A SHAPELY MOUNTAIN, protruding from the line of the Southern Highlands. Callander people refer to it affectionately as 'The Ben', in the same way that Fort William folk refer to Ben Nevis. The name may derive from Ben an Leothaid, meaning 'mountain-of-the-gentle-slope', although Ben le Dia, the 'mountain of God' or 'of light' is far more appropriate. At 2,875ft (879m), it is frequently ascended. Long ago it was the site of an ancient ritual and in this capacity is known as a 'Beltane' hill – La Buidhe (pronounced boo-ee) Bealltuinn, the 'Yellow Day of the Fires of Bel'. On the first day of May, the old Celtic New Year, the young people of the area met on the summit to commemorate an old rite, the lighting of the Bealltuinn fires in celebration of Bel (from Be'uill, 'Life of All'), an early Celtic sun god.

On the lower ground all fires were extinguished before midnight. New sacrificial fires were kindled and hearth fires relit from the purifying hilltop flames. Sometimes cattle were driven between the fires in the belief that this would protect them from disease. On the summit of Ben Ledi, on smooth turf, a bannock (scone) was prepared from oatmeal, eggs and milk. A fire was lit and when it died down the bannock was cooked on a stone set in the ashes. It was then cut into slices, one of which was marked with charcoal. The slices were put in a bonnet and handed round the company: whoever drew the marked portion had to skip three times through the embers to ensure good fortune. Pieces were then tossed into the air as gift tokens to those birds and animals which might harm the flocks and herds – the wolf, fox, eagle, raven and hooded crow.

Opposite: The Bracklinn Falls, near Callander, crash through a narrow gorge

WATERFALLS

THE TWO WATERFALLS close to Callander are not particularly spectacular in summer, but in winter they can be truly fearsome, a huge volume of brown and cream water roaring and rushing down the gorge. For the visitor in summer they are nevertheless still worth a visit. The Bracklinn Falls (given as 'Brackland' in older sources) on the River Kelty and on the fringe of Callander take their name from the Gaelic *braec*, meaning 'speckled' or 'dappled', a reference to water-borne debris and flecked foam. In his novel *Kidnapped*, Robert Louis Stevenson called his Highland hero Alan 'Breck' Stewart, 'Breck' referring to the fact that he had a pock-marked – or speckled – face. Linn means a pool.

These are menacing falls, tumbling through a high-walled and forbidding gorge and surrounded by trees. The word 'Kelty' probably derives from *coilltidh*, meaning 'a wooded place'. The falls are reached by a path from a car park above the golf course. Sir Walter Scott drew on the scene for his novel of the 1745 Rising, *Waverley*, and he rode across the then flimsy bridge for a bet (there is now a new bridge, built by Army engineers). He also made passing reference to the falls in *The Lady of the Lake*, describing the Highland hero Roderick Dhu as 'brave, but wild as Bracklinn's thundering wave'.

Not far away are linking hills, Uamh Mor and Uamh Beag, which contain a hidden ravine where the MacGregors hid stolen cattle. Stevenson also brought Uamh Beag into *Kidnapped*. The modern and busy A84 runs through the wooded and botanically rich Pass of Leny, north of Callander, and many visitors stop at a car park or follow the west bank path to see the Falls of Leny. Take care crossing the road. The name Leny derives from the Gaelic *lanaigh*, meaning 'a boggy place' and the water falls in twin cataracts. Stevenson depicted Alan Breck and David Balfour leaping falls in Glen Coe, but they were probably an amalgam in his mind of Leny, Bracklinn, the Falls of Rogie, near Strathpeffer, and falls in Glen Orchy, in Argyll, all of which he visited.

2 BALQUHIDDER OF THE BRAES:
THE LANDS OF THE CLANS

The Kirkton, Balquhidder, where Rob Roy MacGregor is buried. Loch Voil is on the right

THERE IS PROBABLY NO OTHER area in the southern Highlands which contains so much absorbing history in a relatively small space as the 15 miles (24km) long Glen of Balquhidder. It is a side glen that the busy A84 passes by, but parts of it were once part of the marriage arrangements between James IV and the Welsh princess Margaret Tudor, and its fertile corners were cherished by the Fergussons, Stewarts, MacLarens and MacGregors. The road north from Callander passes through the wooded Pass of Leny, along the shores of Loch Lubnaig and through the forestry village of Strathyre, and there is a sense of being in the real Highlands. Strathyre is dominated by a mound-shaped hill, Ben Shian (Ben an t-Sithein), one of many faery hills which dotted the Highlands, and the village has a memorial to the eighteenth-century Gaelic evangelist Dugald Buchanan who was born there. The River Balvag flows sluggishly from Balquhidder to Loch Lubnaig and the low ground occasionally floods. Local people call this flooding Loch Occasional.

Close to the mouth of the glen and just off the main road is an old inn called Kingshouse: the name harks back to the days when it was a military barracks, a depot for mail and a place where the coach horses were changed. Balquhidder glen runs away westwards, dominated on both sides by high mountains or their outliers which are popular with hill trampers. A narrow road leads to the Kirkton of Balquhidder where there is a nineteenth-century church and the ruins of at least two other older churches. It was here that one of the most grisly episodes in clan history took place. The king's forester in Glen Artney found some MacGregors poaching deer, and he cut their ears off. Their colleagues later waylaid the forester and cut his head off. They took it to Ardvorlich house on the shores of Loch Earn where his sister was married to Stewart of Ardvorlich. She invited them in and gave them food, as is the Highland custom – but when she left the room to get more, they put her brother's head on the table. She was pregnant at the time and the stress of it all caused her to become deranged, and she fled into the hills. The MacGregors then took the head to Balquhidder church and placed it on the altar. They swore they would take the blame collectively, one of several deeds that inflamed monarchs and hostile chiefs.

There were several clan spats here. The MacLarens were powerful, and claimed they had the right to enter church first, and trouble could – and did – break out if that was not respected. They and the Buchanans had the

Road signs direct visitors to the clans glen of Balquhidder

Attractive St Fillans, at the east end of Loch Earn

equivalent of a lager louts' brawl one market day and the MacGregors joined in happily.

The reasonably spry visitor at the Kirkton should walk up the Kirkton Glen to where a large crag can be clearly seen: this is Creag an Tuirc, Crag of the Boar, and it was a gathering place for the MacLarens. There are outstanding views down the length of the glen to Loch Voil and Loch Doine, and Inverlochlarig Beag, where Rob Roy died, can also be picked out. Rob, his wife Mary and sons Coll and Ranald are buried at the Kirkton, and so is the wife of the Rev Robert Kirk, Isobel.

Long passes lead northwards to Glen Dochart and Strath Fillan, to Loch Katrine, Brig o' Turk and to Loch Lubnaig-side. The Stewart glen of Glen Buckie stretches out before the eye: here, undercover agent Dr Archie Cameron, the last Jacobite leader to be executed in Britain (1753), was captured by a Redcoat patrol.

Life was different long ago. Loch Voil had a water beast on the lines of the Loch Ness monster, though it has been very coy in modern times, and the Kirkton Glen is reputed to have a spectral hunter who carries a musket, wears nineteenth-century clothing and is accompanied by two deer hounds. Several sightings of the hunter have been claimed. The Balquhidder Glen contains the stones of the people of pre-history and relics of the Celtic Saint Angus, Church patron of the glen. Several distinguished literary visitors also came here, including Scott, Stevenson and the Wordsworths. In modern times the glen has changed even more markedly, with conifer forestry replacing some of the hill farms, and arable cultivation or grazing becoming less extensive. At one time the little school had forty pupils: now it is closed.

The road down the glen is narrow and ends at a car park close to Inverlochlarig Beag, much used by mountaineers. The mouth of the glen, however, is wide, the A84 leading onwards to Loch Earn. Nowadays the local water-ski championships are held at Loch Earn and there is an award-winning activity centre at Lochearnhead which offers kayaking, canoeing, dinghy sailing, archery and guided walks. For those interested in golf, Loch Earn has thirty-two courses within a two-hour drive.

'Come ye from Balwhither? [former spelling] The name of it makes all there is of me rejoice', says Catriona as she greets David Balfour in Stevenson's sequel to *Kidnapped*.

It's that kind of place.

Above: Fun on the water. Loch Earn is a popular watersports centre

Opposite: The restored castle of Edinample, now a private house, on the shores of Loch Earn

ROB ROY MACGREGOR

ROB ROY MACGREGOR is possibly the best known Highlander of all time... and the most misunderstoood. He is often described as an outlaw (and that is true from the point of view of his enemies), but he was also a heroic leader of a section of his clan, outwitting two dukes and the British Army. Some may find it surprising that he actually died in his bed on 31 January 1734, at Inverlochlarig Beag at the head of Balquhidder glen. He is buried at the old church at the Kirkton of Balquhidder, his grave covered by an ancient Celtic slab stone and now surrounded by small iron railings.

The name 'Roy' derives from the Gaelic ruadh, meaning 'red'. He was born into Clan Alpin or Clan Gregor (the MacGregors) who claimed descent from Scottish monarchs. They owned lands in Glen Strae, near Loch Awe, but fell out with the expansionist Campbells and were pushed eastwards, eventually settling in Balquhidder, the Trossachs, Glen Lyon and around Loch Rannoch. They were pugnacious and greatly angered Scottish monarchs – at one time their name was banned, their children could be taken away and their womenfolk branded. They were forbidden weapons and were not allowed to assemble in any numbers, and a bounty was paid for their heads. But the MacGregors, the 'Children of the Mist', survived.

Rob Roy was born in Glen Gyle, on the shores of Loch Katrine, in the Trossachs. His father was a leading MacGregor and his mother was a Campbell. Rob was renowned for his strength and for his skill with weapons: he was only eighteen when he fought under Viscount Dundee at the battle of Killiecrankie in 1689, the first of the Jacobite battles. The name 'Jacobite' derives from the Latin for James, Jacobus, and applies to families and clans who wanted to put the exiled Stuarts back on the throne of Britain.

He joined the Lennox Watch, a band of clansmen who indulged in blackmail (see Introduction, p.7), and in 1693 he married Mary Campbell of Comer, now a hill farm at the 'back' of Ben Lomond (Sir Walter Scott called her Helen). When the MacGregors' name was banned, Rob Roy took the cover name of Campbell. He was a man of marked organisational ability and a natural leader. He acquired lands at Craigroystan and Inversnaid at Loch Lomond, and rented grazing in Balquhidder. He prospered as a cattle dealer and borrowed cash from the Duke of Montrose and other powerful men to increase his herds. However, disaster struck him because his chief drover absconded with his funds and letters of credit. Powerful enemies falsely accused him of embezzlement and orders were issued for his arrest. He was outlawed and his wife and family evicted from their Craigroystan land by Montrose's factor, Graham of Killearn.

The grave of Highland hero Rob Roy MacGregor at Balquhidder. His wife, Mary, and two sons are also buried there

The Campbell Earl of Breadalbane, who hated Montrose, gave Rob some land in Glen Dochart and from there and in the Trossachs Rob swiped his enemies far and wide, stealing cattle, sheep and goats. He increased his blackmail activities and he several times intervened when poor or unprotected people were being harassed by powerful chiefs and their helpers. He became a much-loved folk hero. He mobilised Clan Gregor for the Jacobite Rising of 1715, leading raids in Lennox, destroying the Clan Colquhoun boats on Loch Lomond and capturing Hanoverian guns. He was accused of

The ruins of two churches can be seen at the Kirkton, Balquhidder

being inactive at the Battle of Sheriffmuir, but modern research – mainly carried out by the late mountaineer and writer W.H. Murray – has shown that, contrary to some reports, he did behave there in an honourable fashion. Finally, he was accused of high treason, and his Glen Dochart house burned by Swiss mercenaries. He had some respite when the Campbell Duke of Argyll allowed him to build a house in Glen Shira, near Inveraray.

The tales about him grew. As well as being persecuted by Montrose, he fell foul of the Duke of Atholl and happily raided the duke's lands. He twice escaped from imprisonment – on one occasion he was tied to a horse while crossing the River Forth, but managed to cut the belt that held him and dived into the water and got away. He was given a royal pardon in 1725 and converted to Catholicism, partly through his links with the Drummond family who had aided him.

People came from all over the Highlands for his funeral and his memory is revered to this day. As Sir Walter Scott put it in an epic song/poem: 'While there's leaves in the forest and foam on the river, MacGregor despite them shall flourish forever.'

3 LOCH VENACHAR AND THE WOOD OF LAMENTATION

ONE OF THE MOST INTRIGUING NAMES in the Trossachs area is the Wood of Lamentation. It lies on the north side of Loch Venachar and alongside the A821 road and is not named as such on the Ordnance Survey map. It is an odd name and has lessons for the modern visitor. Tradition has it that a water sprite inhabited the loch: it took the form of a water horse and lured people, and particularly children, to their deaths – hence the 'Wood of Lamentation'. A more prosaic explanation and one which is of importance to us today is that Scottish lochs often shelve at the edges. This means that the shallow water close to the shore can be tolerably warm, particularly after long periods of sunshine, but the deeper water further out can be very cold and can cause cramp: because of this there have been some tragic drownings in recent years involving people who paddled about at the edge

Above: Silver birches fringe the shores of Loch Venachar

Opposite: Looking across Loch Achray to the holiday complex, An Tigh Mor, in the Trossachs

31

Above: Reflections in the tranquil Loch Achray, in the heart of the Trossachs

Opposite: (top) Loch Achray is a favourite haunt of anglers; (below) Ben Venue and Loch Achray, part of an area made famous by Walter Scott

of the loch because of the congenial water temperature, but have then set out to swim to a further shore or to an island or have gone well out of their depth, and so got into trouble. It may be that mothers long ago said to children: 'Stay away from the waterside or the *each uishge*, the water horse, will get you' and that they did not necessarily believe in the role of such a creature, but were merely trying to steer their children away from risk by effectively frightening them. It is true, of course, that Gaelic lore features many supernatural beings associated with running water, and with lochs and sea lochs and many were believed to foretell death and calamity.

The A821 road westwards from Callander initially passes through scenery which is stark and strong rather than sylvan. Loch Venachar is now a reservoir and has a dam at one end, and its character has changed since Sir Walter Scott scrutinised it and used its head as a muster place for clansmen in *The Lady of the Lake*. It is a popular loch and contains salmon and brown trout; on the north shore boats can be hired for fishing, and its south shore has a sailing club. Its name derives from the Gaelic *bheann-chair*, and has its roots in a time before the loch was dammed. Historian Dr A. MacGregor Hutcheson, the former chairman of the Clan Gregor Society and an expert on place names, explains that although the meaning of the name 'Venachar' is often given as 'pointed', it literally means 'horns cast', a reference to the red deer which each year cast their antlers and grow another set. However, popular usage has applied it to sites where a river bend resembles a broad brow garnished with short horns. Here the 'horns' refer to the remnants of the former course of either the Black Water river at the west end of Loch Venachar or the Eas Gobhain at the east, but when the loch was dammed and it increased in size, the whole topography changed and the origins of this name disappeared below the water surface.

The swelling slopes of Ben Ledi flank the westwards traveller on the north side and lead up from the old farm house of Coilantogle. This was once the most popular route of ascent for 'The Ben' until the Forestry Commission created a car park and way-marked a path from Loch Lubnaig-side. People still ascend from Coilantogle, but car parking there is difficult. The road becomes increasingly shrouded with trees. It passes a farm called Milton, a township which once had a mill and where the novelist Annie S. Swan (1859–1943) once lived late in her life. All her books had strong romantic themes and she was very popular in the 1930s. She drew on Callander and Lochearnhead for her 1913 novel, *The Bridge Builders*.

Opposite: (top) The tiny Trossachs Church is cradled by Loch Achray and Ben A'n. The church is still part of an inhabited parish and has featured in two films; (below) The Loch Achray Hotel, at the foot of Ben Venue, is popular with touring coach parties

Ben Ledi from the shore of Loch Venacher

The further west the road goes, the more the traveller starts to get the feel of the 'real' Trossachs. The wayside knolls become ever more wooded, Brig o' Turk village and the mouth of Glen Finglas are passed – and then the road bends and the traveller is afforded a glorious view of shining Loch Achray with the soaring slopes of Ben Venue as a backcloth. This is a famous view, much commented upon in past times, and in the days of horse-drawn carriages was a favourite stopping place. Alas, the bend is tight and nowadays the coach or car-borne driver is only able to get a quick glimpse whilst endeavouring not to put the vehicle off the road.

Loch Achray is much bigger now as a result of water supply schemes, but although its character has changed it is just as beautiful. Dorothy Wordsworth and Queen Victoria admired it, and Sir Walter Scott (who else?) wrote about it in *The Lady of the Lake*:

> *The Minstrel came once more to view*
> *The eastern ridge of Ben Venue,*
> *For, ere he parted, he would say*
> *Farewell to lovely Loch Achray --*
> *Where shall he find, in foreign land,*
> *So lone a lake, so sweet a strand!*

These last two lines are frequently quoted, although Loch Achray cannot nowadays be called 'lone'. Another snippet of history is that a 'clan spat' – or affray – took place around its shores during the reign of James 1 of Scotland. The keeper of the royal forest there was James Beg Stewart, the son of Murdoch, Duke of Albany, Regent of Scotland, when James I was captive in England. James Beg had a hunting lodge on an island in Loch Achray and on one occasion met some Campbells who were on a hunting expedition. Angry words were exchanged and the Campbells threatened to return – which they did, but on their second visit they were attacked by James Beg's men and forced to flee.

On a grassy knoll overlooking Loch Achray stands one of the most picturesque churches in Scotland, the Trossachs Church, dedicated to St Kessog, and now a living Church of Scotland kirk. The site was chosen by Lady Willoughby d'Eresby a century ago, one of the Ancaster family who were prominent in this area. It looks exactly as many visitors think a Highland church should look. Services and weddings are still held there and it has figured in at least two films. It caught Queen Victoria's approving eye and she wrote about it in her diary.

Scott's writings did an enormous amount to draw attention to this area and two major business concerns are testimony to his influence: the modern and extended Loch Achray hotel at the foot of Ben Venue, nowadays a hotel very popular with coach parties, and the massive, baronial-style (former) Trossachs Hotel nearby, distinguished by its towers and impressive frontage. The latter was built in 1852, replacing an older inn, a development which caused great anger and complaint amongst visitors. Amongst its more distinguished guests were the American novelist Nathaniel Hawthorne and the playwright J.M. Barrie. In more recent years it lost trade and fell into disrepair and for a time was quite dilapidated. However, it has now been rebuilt and given a new identity. Renamed the Tigh Mor (Big House), it is now a thriving holiday property complex. This is good news and it stands as a fitting monument to the success of tourism in the Trossachs.

The A821 now takes on a double character, with one leg heading west for Loch Katrine and the other running southwards on a route which has another evocative name, the Duke's Pass. All of this is the heart of the Trossachs.

4 Monarchs and Artists: Brig o' Turk and Glen Finglas

AN ARTIST STOOD ON A ROCK looking at a Highland burn tumbling over boulders and stones and fringed by a canopy of trees... and his eyes also rested on the wife of another man. Illicit love was to blossom in an atmosphere of friendship, of walking expeditions, of rejoicing in the sunlight and muttering in the rain, of revelling in the beauties of the landscape and of helping create memorable drawings and paintings. This arena of slumbering passion is called Glen Finglas (also given as Finlas) which lies seven miles (11km) from Callander and runs northwards from Brig o' Turk village into a range of hills which separates the Trossachs from Balquhidder of the Braes. Here a love affair developed last century which involved two of the best known men in England and whose Scottish holiday was to change their lives forever. It was to be the biggest marital scandal since the time of Lord Byron, which is saying something.

In the summer of 1853, the essayist and art and social critic John Ruskin (1819–1900) came to Brig o' Turk with his wife Euphemia Gray and his friend, the artist (Sir) John Everett Millais (1829–96). Millais had helped to form a 'school' called the pre-Raphaelite brotherhood, a group of English painters who, broadly speaking, took their ideals from the paintings of Italian masters before Raphael, the famous Italian Renaissance painter and architect who died in 1520. They were noted for elaborate detail, bright colours and outdoor settings. Brig o' Turk and Glen Finglas had a reputation for sylvan beauty which attracted Millais.

The Ruskins stayed in a cottage in the glen and Millais lodged at an inn in Brig o' Turk. The painter's brother, William, accompanied him, and so did Ruskin's friend, the physician Sir Henry Ackland, for a time. Ruskin had begun to write his *Lectures on Architecture and Painting* which he was to deliver in Edinburgh, and he also did some sketching. He wrote in his diary that he had been drawing on the rocks by the burn, the Finglas Water. He praised a Trossachs sunset: 'The skies all turquoise and violet, melted in dew and heavenly bars of delicate cloud behind Ben Venue in evening.'

Millais erected a tent in the glen where he worked on a famous full-

Glen Finglas reservoir covers ground where kings once hunted

37

The cattle drovers of the past took their herds through Glen Finglas

length portrait of Ruskin, bareheaded, against a background of trees and crags. Some local people today can identify the individual sites in the painting, and in other drawings and paintings, although a modern dam has altered the flow of the burn. Millais was jovial and happy and painted 'Pre-Raphaelite Emporium' on his tent. He wrote to a friend: 'We have immense enjoyment painting out on the rocks, and having our dinner brought to us there, and in the evening climbing up the steep mountains for exercise, Mrs Ruskin accompanying us.' They wore muslin masks or face scarves, like the Invisible Man in the television serial of that name, to keep the midgies at bay.

Sometimes they had bad weather, but they were undeterred. Millais wrote to a friend (referring to Millais' brother, William): 'The last four days we have had incessant rain, swelling the streams to torrents. This afternoon we all walked to see some of the principal waterfalls which in colour resemble XXX Stout. The roads are deeper in water than the Wandle, so we were walking ankle deep. The dreariness of the mountainous country in wet weather is beyond everything. I have employed myself making little studies of Mrs Ruskin whilst William has given way to whisky and execrastion.'

The 'little sketches' of Mrs Ruskin led to yearning eyes and meaningful glances: on the surface all was normal, but underneath Millais and Effie had fallen in love. Ruskin did not seem to notice, or if he had he did not seem to mind. He wrote in his diary: 'Out with Millais at six, holding the umbrella over him while he worked, and watching the stream, looking down it, due south.'

A few weeks later Millais left and returned to England. The following year Effie's marriage to Ruskin was annulled and it soon became known that the marriage had not been consumated. Soon after she married Millais, and the couple's story is now an indelible part of the history of one of the Trossachs most changed glens.

Brig o' Turk was also to become a haunt for other artists, including the group known as 'the Glasgow boys'. (Sir) James Guthrie was one of these, and his painting *A Funeral Service in the Highlands* is based on a scene at Brig o' Turk. The name 'Finglas' is reputed to mean 'fair green glen' because the grass is supposed to take on a bleached appearance in winter. The village of Brig o' Turk was first brought to the attention of the general public by Sir Walter Scott. He wrote in *The Lady of the Lake*:

> *And when the Brigg of Turk was won*
> *the foremost horseman rode alone.*

The glen is still attractively wooded and the white cottages are still strung out on either side, but the building of new houses and the reservoir higher up the glen have changed the village's character and lessened the flow of the burn. The cataracts and pools, although still beautiful, have lost some of their zest since Millais painted there, and the dam and an estate track in a linking glen have tamed the landscape somewhat. The village inn was visited by Queen Victoria in 1869 and is now a dwelling house; a later inn was burned down. The original village was a township huddled around a ford over the Finglas Water where an old causeway ran. There was once a bridge

This tea room in Brig o' Turk, at the mouth of Glen Finglas, provides sustenance for many walkers and cyclists

Top: Ferns form a carpet of lush growth in Glen Finglas and the Trossachs as a whole
Above: Mosses and other vegetation provide delicate and complex colours throughout the area

made of wood: the present stone bridge dates from the start of this century. This writer once explained to a group of overseas visitors that the name 'Turk' derived from the Gaelic for a boar, *tuirc*, because Scottish kings hunted in this area. There was a pause and a voice said: 'No, I wanted to know what "brig" meant!' (It is the Scots word for a bridge; in Gaelic it is 'Drochaid an Tuirc'.)

The modern village has changed from a population almost exclusively devoted to crofting, forestry and hill farming, to one that includes people who commute to Callander, Stirling and further afield. A cafe at the entrance to the glen is busy with hillwalkers and mountain bikers who have come over the long passes from Balquhidder and Loch Katrine-side, and not far from the bridge itself a modern restaurant is housed in older buildings at Duncraggan. A primary school still flourishes: older pupils go by bus to McLaren High School in Callander. It was at Duncraggan that Scott, in *The Lady of the Lake*, depicted Malise, the bearer of the Fiery Cross (used as a signal to summon the clan), as he burst in on the mourners lamenting the death of Duncan and handed over the cross to his son Angus, the new chieftain. As Sir Walter rode around he noted site after site for this memorable poem. Another noted site was Lendrick House, just to the east of Brig o' Turk, once a hunting lodge of the Earls of Moray. In modern times it has become a youth hostel and latterly a retreat centre.

The modern reservoir is large and occupies most of the upper part of the glen. A side glen, Gleann Casaig, reputed to have been the site of an ecclesiastical centre and which takes its name from St Kessog, runs northeast towards a ridge which connects Ben Ledi and Stuc Dubh (Black Point). One of the most intriguing names in the area lies at the crest of this ridge: Lochan nan Corp, the 'small loch of the dead'. An ancient local tradition says that the ice on this lochan broke under the weight of a funeral party carrying a coffin to St Bride's chapel, at the south end of Loch Lubnaig, and all were drowned. However, it is perhaps more likely that the name simply derives from the fact that the lochan lies at the crest of a well known pass which was used as a coffin route. Another glen, called Meann – 'of the young roes' – branches off from Glen Finglas and becomes a key pass running north. There is an old burial ground dedicated to St Kessog here. Plans by the Woodland Trust to plant upper Glen Finglas with deciduous trees will do much to restore its old face. The traveller staring up the glen sees the hill ground dominated by a large, bold-fronted hill called Meall Cala, meaning 'hill of the entry' – this is indeed appropriate because it splits the passes leading over to Loch Katrine-side and Balquhidder.

Glen Finglas is a quiet glen nowadays, but it is packed with saga and legend and this adds greatly to the enjoyment of discerning visitors. It was a glen of the Stewarts and they had an old tradition of keeping one household fire alight winter and summer – and they undoubtedly kept the Beltane ceremonies on Ben Ledi (see p. 9), too. An old story has it that last century during a time of cattle plague the people did extinguish this fire, and then kindled another by rubbing a beam in a barn with a piece of wood in the hope that this pure flame, with its links with ancient fire worship, would help to protect them. The glen used to have a great deal of juniper, and during an outbreak of plague in the 1500s it was burned three times a day to keep the disease away. These passes have known packmen who carried items of clothing, tools and knick-knacks (and gossip) to the glen communities. They have also seen the passage of the cattle drovers and whisky smugglers. Much of this illicit spirit was made on Loch Tay-side and then taken to the burgeoning city of Glasgow where a clear profit could be made.

Sir Walter visited Glen Finglas and it may have helped influence him to write *The Lady of the Lake*. He was greatly taken by the work of James 'Ossian' MacPherson (1738–96) who claimed to have discovered a hoard of ancient Gaelic poetry. Scott also wrote a ballad called *Glenfinlas*; sub-titled *Lord Ronald's Coronach* (a coronach is a lament). It tells of a fatal hunting expedition. Scott's friend, James Hogg, the Ettrick Shepherd, was so taken with this poem that when he travelled through the Trossachs he made a point of visiting the glen.

Sir Walter was keenly interested in the supernatural and particularly as expressed in the folk tradition of faeries, goblins, brownies, water horses and other spectres. The glen has a faery knoll, Cnoc nan Sidheag, and Scott maintained that one translation of Glenfinlas was 'the glen of the green women'. He wrote that these spectral beings and other faeries wore green and were irritated when mortals wore the same colour and it was considered to be particularly unlucky when green was worn by some families and clans, including the local family of the Grahams. In *The Lady of the Lake* he also makes Glen Finglas the site of a ritual to divine the future, called the Taighairn: a person wishing to resolve an issue that was worrying him/her was wrapped in the skin of a newly slain bullock and placed beside a waterfall, or at the bottom of a precipice, or in some other wild spot where the scenery was forbidding and grim; he/she then tried to resolve this issue by concentrating the mind and drawing on the inspiration of the spirits who inhabited such places.

Colourful foxgloves contrast with the grey rocks of the Trossachs

Another local tale relates how two travellers were once accosted by two beautiful maidens in Glen Finglas: one was lured away, the other closed his eyes and prayed. The one who was lured away was later found with his throat torn out. There's a moral there somewhere.

Campbell Nairne, author of the excellent guide book *The Trossachs* produced in 1981, told of a certain Brig o' Turk man called Parlan (pronounced farlan) MacFarlane: this Parlan was totally immersed in Gaelic culture and was convinced there was a spectral water bull in Loch Katrine. He told Dr D.W.Watson, Professor of Celtic at Edinburgh University, that he had not seen it himself, but he had seen the calf.

The waters of the new dam bury much of what was once royal hunting ground and which was within a day's horse ride from Stirling. The royal foresters, generally men of power and rank, often had their hands full trying to capture poachers. When James VI of Scotland went down to London to become James I of England at the Union of the Crowns in 1603 the raiding increased, the greater distance between the king and his properties effectively reducing his authoritative influence and control. He was informed in 1607 that there was 'verie grete spoyle' of his game and deer, and he sent an angry message to his foresters instructing them to be more diligent. In those days taking someone else's cattle, and poaching generally, were in fact considered more of a manly sport than an offence, except to the monarch or laird who punished poachers severely, sentences ranging from ear cropping to hanging. However, records tell us that in 1611 the men of Glen Gyle, Loch Katrine-side, Balquhidder and Strathyre – probably mainly MacGregors – came almost every day armed with guns, bows and other weapons and killed the king's deer. James, the Earl of Moray, who was appointed hereditary keeper, tried to arrest the leaders and put them before the Privy Council, but they escaped and were declared outlaws.

Glen Finglas is indeed peaceful nowadays when compared to these colourful and turbulent times.

New power from the glens: the Glen Finglas reservoir aids production of electricity

The Finglas Water is greatly loved by artists for its beauty and movement

5 LOCH KATRINE AND THE BRISTLY GROUND

LOCH KATRINE, in the heart of the Trossachs, is remarkable in that although the hand of human beings is clearly laid upon the landscape, it is still undeniably beautiful and often wild. Dozens of cars and coaches now park at the Trossachs pier at the east end of the loch. At one time there was a natural barrier of heaped-up rocks here, scaled by using the roots of trees like a ladder and sometimes with a helping rope attached. Sir Walter Scott described it in *The Lady of the Lake* thus:

> *Where the rude (rough) Trosachs' dread defile*
> *Opens on Katrine's lake and isle.*

This barrier was dynamited out of the way when the Victorian engineers and Glasgow Corporation began their mammoth scheme to pipe Loch Katrine's pure water 35 miles (56km) to the city of Glasgow. The water was so soft that the consumption of soap apparently dropped by half in the industrial city, such was the cleansing effectiveness of the water alone. It is also a loch which rarely freezes. Hillwalkers sometimes follow the line of the pipelines through

Glen Gyle where Rob Roy was born

Below: Scott's Pool, on the Ledard burn near Loch Ard, was greatly loved by Sir Walter Scott

the woods today because they are now of some significance in industrial archaeology. The landowners of the time did not want their sylvan retreats spoiled and it has to be said that, on the whole, the water supply planners did a reasonably satisfactory conservation job. Natural stone was used for walls and buildings and iron railings were painted black and were both substantial and relatively unobtrusive.

The water level has been raised more than once and some historic sites have inevitably changed. The 'Silver Strand' of white pebbles which Sir Walter mentions in his poem vanished when the water was raised in 1895, and the wooded island of Eilean Molach – the 'shaggy island' – which features in the poem as Ellen's Isle, is much smaller than in the past. The Silver Strand is commemorated in a famous painting by the artist Horatio McCulloch. Sir Walter's poem greatly boosted visitor figures. People used to travel to the area book in hand and stand and argue about the exact location of the place names. In the first part of the poem the hunted stag finds safety in 'the deep Trossachs wildest nook'.

The modern local and water authorities have done their best to protect Loch Katrine's beauty and have largely succeeded, although some of the hydro-electric pylons can grate on the eye. There is a visitor centre sited at the Trossachs pier, with display material about the water scheme. There is also a cafe, toilets and a shop, and bikes can be hired here too.

The meaning of the name Katrine (pronounced 'kat-rin') is open to several theories: it may derive from a woman's name, or it may mean 'of the furies', or 'of the torment' (both linked to legend); alternatively, it may come from cateran meaning a 'raider', 'robber' or 'reiver'. All of the lochside and part of long Strath Gartney was once MacGregor territory, and any person cycling or walking on the north side of the loch today passes many sites which once knew the tramp of the feet of Rob Roy MacGregor and his people. (The road on the north side is closed to public cars.)

Scott's poem includes stirring scenes of Clan Alpin (the MacGregors) going to war. Records tell us that soldier Adam Ferguson, serving under Wellington in the Peninsular War against Napoleon, received extra rations for reading the poem aloud and on one occasion read the battle scene to keep his company steady under fire. The effect of this poem was astonishing. The landowning Ancaster family had a kind of replica bower built on Ellen's Isle, with walls and window frames made from latticed branches, moss and fern floors, a wooden table and chairs. Weapons, including a sword which allegedly belonged to Rob Roy, and deer skins hung on the walls. Alas, that modern scourge, vandalism, operated even then: the bower was repeatedly tarnished by visitors leaving their picnic rubbish and was eventually accidentally set on fire. The Duchess of Perth also had a bower like a watchtower created on top of one of the knolls close to the (now) pier.

There is no road on the south side of the eight miles (13km)-long loch. The car driver can reach Stronachlachar (which means 'stone-mason's point') at the west end of the loch by driving on a minor road off the B829,

The Trossachs pier, the starting point for a boat trip up Loch Katrine

the Aberfoyle to Inversnaid road. A popular steamer sails regularly up Loch Katrine, sometimes stopping at Stronachlachar where passengers can stretch their legs and cyclists can disembark; some sailings turn part-way up the loch. The east end is the best in giving the feel of the past, the boat nosing out between a series of richly wooded little islands and headlands. Small bluffs and a thick covering of heather typify the area – Dorothy Wordsworth, sister of poet William, praised the mixture of rock, heather and trees when she wrote about their visit to the Trossachs in August 1803. She and William met up with their friend, the poet Samuel Taylor Coleridge, on the shores of Loch Katrine and he hailed them with a shout 'exhulting in the glory of Scotland'. The Wordsworths were initially sniffy about Loch Katrine and considered it inferior to Ullswater, in the Lake District, but the area gradually grew upon them. In past times passengers disembarked at Stronachlachar where there used to be an hotel and ponies took them to Inversnaid.

The story of the tourism boats on the loch is an entertaining one. As the popularity of the area grew, tourists were rowed up the loch in an eight-oared galley, *The Water Witch*, manned by costumed Highlanders. There was great rivalry between it and the first steamer on the loch, *The Gypsy*, taken there by road from Stirling in the early summer of 1843, having got temporarily stuck en route. It was manned by a captain and a crew of three and made its maiden voyage the day after its arrival. Both crews decided on the same departure time – and to the chagrin of the steamer, *The Water Witch*

Loch Katrine from Ben Venue

beat the steamer for speed. Competition for the tourism trade went on for a week – and then at dead o' night *The Gypsy* disappeared from her moorings and was later found sunk. The police were sent for and the Loch Katrine boatmen appeared in court before the sheriff at Dunblane. They were not co-operative and insisted on speaking Gaelic, and an interpreter had to be summoned. But no evidence against them could be found and some of them or their friends put it about that a 'faery water-bull' had done it and they were released. At the close of the case one newspaper called the sinking 'an act characteristic of a former age, and a disgrace to the present' – clearly the spirit of Rob Roy still lingered. But steam eventually won, and the Loch Lomond Steamboat Company put a bigger and faster vessel on the loch and called it *Rob Roy*. It was carried over in sections from Inversnaid. Its successor, another *Rob Roy*, carried Queen Victoria and Prince Albert on the loch.

The old Glasgow Corporation water department brought the present steamer, the *Sir Walter Scott*, to the loch in 1900; it has a crew of seven and can carry 400 passengers and it is the only surviving screw steamer in regular passenger service in Scotland. Built by William Denny & Brothers Ltd at Dumbarton, it retains its original engines. These are powered by steam using smokeless solid fuel, and engine buffs are happy to peer at them for hours. The steamer was taken in sections up Loch Lomond by barge and then overland by horse and cart from Inversnaid to Stronachlachar. It is of a type built for the rivers and lakes of countries once part of the British Empire (and now the Commonwealth). It was launched on 31 October 1899.

The big farms the visitor sees from the boat on the north side of the loch stand on the site of old holdings and still retain their ancient names – places such as Edra, where the Duke of Perth's standard bearer came from in the 1745 Jacobite Rising. The journeying James Hogg, the Ettrick Shepherd, writer and friend of Scott, praised the fertility of the ground here, and also commented on trees being hacked down to make way for sheep. It is often said that one of these farms, Brenachoil, was where Dr Archie Cameron, the last Jacobite to be executed in Britain, was captured, but in fact this event took place in Glen Buckie, in Balquhidder, and the Redcoat commander's report is quite specific regarding the site. However, in such a Jacobite area there would be a number of safe houses and Dr Cameron was probably given refuge at Brenachoil.

When the troops of General Monck, Cromwell's hatchetman in Scotland, were stamping around this area, some women and children took refuge on Ellen's Isle. A sergeant saw that they had taken

The steamer, the Sir Walter Scott, *sets out for Loch Katrine from the Trossachs pier*

all the boats over to the island and set out to swim there and retrieve the boats so as to make the women accessible to the soldiers. But as he landed, one of the women leaped forward and dirked (stabbed) him to death, and no one else dared follow on.

During the seventeenth-century Scottish Wars of the Covenant, when James Graham, Marquis of Montrose, tried to win Scotland for Charles I, a minor skirmish took place at the east end of Loch Katrine, and a much bigger one on the fringe of Callander. The MacGregors were involved in all of these wars. People were hardy then – they had to be because they were surrounded by powerful enemies and the MacGregors' pugnacious behaviour had incurred the hostility of Scottish monarchs. Yet their own Gaelic culture of songs, stories, piping and the clarsach flourished and learning was respected; it is significant in this respect that Rob Roy's house contained several books. After the MacGregors defeated the Colquhouns at the battle of Glen Fruin (on the west side of Loch Lomond) in 1602, James V1 (who had asked the Colquhouns to be a kind of peace-keeping force) decided to punish them. The Privy Council finally got round to it in about 1611 following further acts of belligerence and self-preservation by the MacGregors. Boats were ordered to be carried from Loch Lomond to Loch Katrine, but the MacGregors fortified the islands and the punitive expedition fizzled out.

The visitor at Stronachlachar will see several offshore islands. One is known locally as the Factor's Island and although sources differ, the story goes that Rob Roy marooned Graham of Killearn, evil factor and kinsman to the Duke of Montrose, on one of these, and relieved him of the rents he had been collecting. Rob made Killearn write to the Duke saying that he, Rob, demanded the cancellation of a debt he owed the Duke and compensation for the burning of two of his houses. The letter is extant, dated 19 November 1716. There was no reply, so Rob kept the money.

Cyclists relax at Stronachlachar pier on Loch Katrine

Rob Roy was born in Glen Gyle (the forked glen), an arm of the modern loch stretching northwards and which is an old pass over to Glen Falloch and Loch Lomond-side. A mainly modern white house can be seen on the east side of this arm, used by shepherds and water department employees and a MacGregor burial ground is situated here; it is sometimes visited by walkers and cyclists. Dorothy Wordsworth and friends stayed there with a family called MacFarlane and Dorothy wrote that the people were 'handsome, healthy and happy-looking'. James Hogg also wrote about going up this pass (called the Parlan Pass and pronounced 'farlan'), and in particular that he fell asleep. When he woke up eagles were circling just above his head. The pass was used by packmen bringing herring from the west coast, and also by the tinkers, the travelling people. There is a small hill loch, Lochan a' Cheard, on the south side of Loch Katrine, nowadays called the Loch of the Tinker.

There is a strong tradition of a community of women, possibly nuns, living in upper Glen Gyle at a place called Kilnacallich. They were best known for being instrumental in the settling of disputes, particularly among the cattle drovers.

Portnellan on Loch Katrine

Over the years the water authority has shown great sensitivity towards MacGregor sites; at Portnellan, for instance, just to the east of Glen Gyle, old MacGregor graves have been re-sited on a little promontory to save them from the waters of the loch when the water level was raised. They were once sited in a sloping field by the water's edge and have been moved twice. Many of the gravestones are very weathered; they date from 1609. Entry is through a little archway and it is altogether an evocative spot and worth walking round to see (cars not allowed). Wordsworth was erroneously told that Rob Roy was buried there and wrote a poem about him. This end of Loch Katrine is also reached by an old coffin route known as the Bealach nan Corp, the Pass of the Bodies. It runs over the hills from Balquhidder and is a popular trek amongst hillwalkers.

Modern visitors looking at the map will see the name 'Royal Cottage' on the south shore of the loch. This commemorates the visit in October 1859 by Queen Victoria and Prince Albert when they came to open the water project. It was renovated in case they wanted to stay overnight, but they confined their stay there to having a meal. Historian and writer Louis Stott has commented that the Loch Katrine aqueduct and the 'underground goblins' of Ben Venue may have prompted Jules Verne, who visited the loch in 1859, to write his adventure story *Les Indes Noires* (*The Black Diamonds*) which is set in – or rather under – the Trossachs: an underground city is hewn out of coal and lit by electricity and some of the detail in it definitely smacks of the

water supply project. Visitors to the Kelvingrove Art Gallery and Museum in Glasgow should have a wander in the adjacent parkland, because there is a huge statue commemorating the arrival of Loch Katrine's water in Glasgow. The city fathers might have crowned it with a statue of the provost or a worthy bailie or the chief engineer, but they chose instead to cap it with Scott's *The Lady of the Lake*, Ellen Douglas. Who said planners have no soul?

As the steamer goes westwards from the Trossachs pier, a great huddle of boulders can be seen at the side of Ben Venue and a little pass runs to where the modern spur-road comes in from the Trossachs road junction. This pass is called the Bealach nam Bo, the Pass of the Cattle, and was used by the MacGregors to take their cattle to the great trysts (fairs) at Crieff and Falkirk; in times past the economy of the Highlands was based on cattle. In more modern times, timber, bark and charcoal were taken from Loch Katrine-side and native iron ore was worked. West of Scotland Water are to restore some of the native woodlands, which will add to the beauty of the loch's shores. The pass was also used by the MacGregors when they had taken someone else's cattle and were hurrying them through into their mountain fastnesses. The Wordsworths, too, visited this pass and William climbed towards the higher slopes of Ben Venue, leaving Dorothy behind. This corner inspired him to write the sonnet called *The Trossachs*. When on the modern steamer it is evocative to reflect that this loch once heard the creak of the oars of the MacGregors' birlinns (galleys), and the swish of their small skiffs, and the rowing songs of the men.

A large huddle of rocks on the loch side of Ben Venue forms part of a corrie in the hill called the 'Goblins Corrie' or the 'Corrie nan Uruisgean' (a corrie is cauldron-shaped, and a common feature of Scottish hills). It is not clear who these mysterious beings were, but they were allegedly supernatural, rather like brownies, who could perform kindly tasks – or were just as likely to turn against you if you were not well disposed towards them. It was a Highland custom to put out milk or oatcake for them, or others in the faery world, and this writer knows some people who still do that. It may be that the goblins or 'Uruisks' are the remnants of an almost forgotten historical event when invaders drove the small people of the hills deeper into mountain refuges; it may also have been true, some writers say, of a kind of Druidic cult. A faery story may mask a real event. Scott wrote in *The Lady of the Lake*:

> *High on the south, huge Benvenue*
> *Down on the lake in masses threw*
> *Crags, knolls and mounds, confusedly hurl'd*
> *The fragments of an earlier world.*

He depicted the Goblins' Corrie as a retreat for Ellen Douglas and her father after they had withdrawn from Roderick Dhu's stronghold on an island in Loch Katrine. In fact Scott's mark is indelibly on this loch and it is entirely appropriate that the modern steamer bears his name.

The Trossachs area is rich in plant life, with an abundance of foxgloves and lichens

Opposite: Rhododendrons, an imported species, show their bright flowers in season at Stronachlachar, at the west end of Loch Katrine

6 Faeries and Forestry: Aberfoyle and the Lands of Menteith

IN THE SAME WAY THAT ROME is remembered because it is 'set on seven hills' and the north-east whisky centre of Dufftown because it is 'set on seven stills', then the forestry village of Aberfoyle will be recollected because it is dominated by six mounds. There are several mounds, of course, but the main ones are the wooded knoll of Doon Hill (the Rev Robert Kirk's faery hill), Lime Craig and the southerly end of the Menteith Hills; soaring Creag More, the 'big crag', which was used by the MacGregors as a sentinel hill; the lower shelf with the Queen Elizabeth Forest Park visitor centre; the knoll where the prominent Covenanters Inn is situated; and towering Ben Lomond far off to the west. The village has the character of a Highland village even though it is not really in the Highlands, but on the fringes, being only 30 miles (48km) from Glasgow and 16 miles (26km) from Stirling. It is split into four main areas and has adequate tourism parking space. It is now home to the Scottish Wool Centre and a new information centre and there are several gift shops specialising in tourism souvenirs and Scottish woollens. The Wool Centre sometimes has additional attractions such as sheepdog displays and

Above: Wooded hills surround the village of Aberfoyle

Opposite: Hidden Loch Drunkie shows a shy face on the Achray Forest Drive

Overleaf: Loch Drunkie is a pleasant place to stroll or picnic

The Trossachs Discovery Centre, an information point for visitors, is sited in the forestry village of Aberfoyle

The Scottish Wool Centre in Aberfoyle often features traditional crafts, such as weaving

Scottish music. It was once linked by rail to the large slate quarry close to the nearby Duke's Pass road, the A821.

The visitor approaching Aberfoyle from the east passes below the Menteith Hills and forestry plantations where an old township called Braeval was once sited. The name means 'the steep slope of the township'. An attractive path runs alongside the hills and descends to the shores of Loch Venachar and the 'back road' into Callander. This walk passes a small lochan which has been created in modern times by drainage from the plantations. An American visitor of Scots descent, Doug Caldow, took a group of American and Canadian walkers through here each year and they saw the lochan grow from nothing to something deserving a name, so they called it Lochan Caldow and so it has remained ever since. When the path descends to Loch Venachar-side the walker is on a private road (for vehicles) leading to a (private) house called 'Invertrossachs'; walking on this road back towards Callander poses no problem. In fact, this name is entirely bogus and the house is really called Drunkie Lodge. However, it was thought that this conjured up unfortunate connections with drink. There is also a Loch Drunkie which can be seen from the Duke's Pass road. Queen Victoria visited Drunkie House in 1869.

Close to Braeval, Aberfoyle golf course comes into view and signs and houses quickly tell the visitor that the modern Aberfoyle is a forestry village. The Milton area to the west was, as the name implies, a place where a prominent mill was sited, and some buildings there have now been restored. The Clachan of Aberfoyle was sited around a famous inn at the west of the modern village; to the south lies the Kirkton, reached over the famous old hump-backed bridge across the River Forth. At that point the river is really quite substantial, far removed from the tiny burn of its beginnings. The Forth starts in the burns to the east of the Ben Lomond watershed and joins up with the River Teith just above Stirling. The village was never of great strategic importance because warring armies and cattle drovers knew they could cross the Forth at the Fords of Frew, nearer to Stirling, and in past times it was only formed by the old Clachan, but its separate parts are gelling effectively nowadays. It has attractive corners and is sited just below the meeting place of the two main burn-rivers which form the Forth: the Duchray Water from the eastern slopes of Ben Lomond, and the Avon-Dhu (Black Water) from Loch Ard. The name 'Aberfoyle' comes from the Gaelic *abar a'phuill*, meaning 'mouth of the muddy pool'.

The great modern woods of the Loch Ard Forest run almost as far as the village of Drymen, though they are split by the lovely Duchray Water and prominent Loch Ard. A clan spat took place in this corner in 1671 when at a christening the Grahams of Duchray and the followers of the Earl of Airth fell out with one another. The old Aberfoyle church, where the christening took place, is now in ruins. It was once linked to Inchmahome priory on the Lake of Menteith.

The kirkyard at the Kirkton contains iron coffins and two heavy mort-safes, used to stop people stealing bodies and selling them to medical researchers. Amongst the gravestones is one dated 1692 for the Rev Robert Kirk who was born in Aberfoyle manse and there is also one for the Rev Patrick Graham (1756–1835), author, historian and friend of Scott, who wrote the first guide to the district. This road to the Kirkton also leads to part of the Loch Ard Forest where there are walking and cycle routes. Visitors to the Trossachs and its fringes, and particularly in the Duchray woods, may see the remains of Nissen huts. These are store buildings generally made of corrugated iron, the walls and roof making one curved piece in the manner of a modern pig arc, on a brick or concrete base. Some are still used for agricultural purposes, but most are no more than a foundation partly hidden by moss, grass and other vegetation in the woods. During World War II these woods were a mammoth munitions base and the huts contained live ammunition, shells and mortar bombs.

Peaceful reflections in Loch Ard

The MacGregors knew Aberfoyle well and if they returned today they would be astonished at the extent of the conifer woodlands. During the Jacobite Rising of 1745 the MacGregors marched through Aberfoyle wearing Jacobite white cockades in their bonnets and blowing kisses to the girls. For its duration they occupied Doune Castle, between Callander and Stirling, which the Jacobites used as a prison for Hanoverian supporters. Sir Walter Scott drew on fact when he portrayed the Aberfoyle inns as favourite places for the MacGregors. The old Baillie Nicol Jarvie Hotel drew its name from Scott's novel *Rob Roy*, although in modern times it has been renovated as flats. The fictional baillie set a Highlander's plaid on fire with a red hot coulter (plough blade), a model of which hung on the outside walls for years. Scott made his preliminary notes for *Rob Roy* in the manse at Aberfoyle. Another literary connection is with the Jacobite poet William Glen, who was born near Aberfoyle and wrote the song *Wae's Me For Prince Charlie*, once taught in many Scottish schools and still sung by modern folk groups.

The magnificent head of a Scottish Black Face Sheep

Iron smelting was carried on in Aberfoyle for a time, and the nearby knoll, Lime Craig, which has spectacular views to the big hills of the north, had a quarry where lime was procured as a fertiliser and as a coating for walls.

The name Covenanters Inn tends to make people think of seventeenth-century Scottish Covenanters who staunchly adhered to their Presbyterian faith even when persecuted; however, the name is modern. In the spring of 1949 a group of Scottish Nationalists, led by Dr John McCormick, met in the inn for two days and launched a petition called the Second Covenant which pledged the signatories to secure a devolved Scottish Parliament, something that has come to pass in our own day. The Covenant was eventually signed by two million people and after the movement gained national publicity the inn, formerly called the Inchrie Hotel, was renamed the Covenanters Inn. The declaration was called the Second Covenant after the famous National Covenant of 1638, a religious and political manifesto which opposed Charles I's attempts to dilute the Presbyterian way of worship of most Scottish Protestants. The National Covenant is one of the most significant events in Scottish history because it had 'national declaration' status. The term Covenant is Biblical in origin, and chosen deliberately for that reason, to emphasise the importance of what was being declared.

The famous Stone of Scone (also known as the Stone of Destiny) – or a duplicate – taken from Scotland by Edward I of England during the fourteenth century and later deposited in Westminster Abbey, was hidden in the Covenanters Inn for a time after it was taken from the abbey by Scottish Nationalists in 1950. It is arguable whether Edward got the real stone during his invasions of Scotland and he may have been palmed off with a dud. Some writers say the stone hidden in the inn was a decoy, others that the one taken from Westminster Abbey was indeed hidden there. However, the current stone has a strong symbolic character and is now placed alongside the Scottish Crown Jewels, the Honours of Scotland, in Edinburgh Castle.

THE REVEREND ROBERT KIRK

ABERFOYLE VILLAGE, now a forestry centre, might be called the faery capital of Scotland, largely due to the work and research of the Rev Robert Kirk, the famous folklorist, who was the Episcopalian minister from 1685 to 1692. He was a noted scholar, the first to translate the metrical psalms into Gaelic, and he was asked to superintend the production of the most significant Gaelic bible of the seventeenth century. He was also involved in the revision of a printed version of the Catechism in Gaelic. He was the seventh son of the minister of Aberfoyle, James Kirk, and after studying divinity at St Andrew's University, he took a Master of Arts degree at Edinburgh University. He became minister at Balquhidder in 1664, and eventually succeeded his father in 1685 when he moved to the manse in Aberfoyle. His first wife, Isobel Campbell, by whom he had a son, died in 1680 and is buried in Balquhidder kirkyard. He later married again and his second wife, Margaret Campbell of Glendaruel, bore him another son and was pregnant when he died; this baby was a girl, Marjorie.

The grave of the Rev Robert Kirk at Aberfoyle, the man who told the faeries secrets

It was Robert Kirk's habit to go daily to the tree-covered mound called Doon Hill, on the fringe of Aberfoyle, behind the old parish church. It was known as a faery knoll and probably takes its name from dun, a fort, which was once sited there. He died on the hill in 1692, probably from a heart attack, although local tradition says he was spirited away by the faeries because they were annoyed at him revealing their lifestyle in a book he wrote called *The Secret Commonwealth*. Its full title is in fact *Secret Commonwealth or an Essay on the Nature and Actions of the Subterranean (and for the most part) Invisible People heretofore going under the names of Fauns and Fairies, or the like, among the Low Country Scots as described by those who have second sight, 1691*. However, it is generally just called *The Secret Commonwealth*.

The faeries allegedly substituted a changeling, which explains why Mr Kirk has a grave in the old kirkyard at the Kirkton of Aberfoyle. Another local tradition maintains that he is still in office and that all successive ministers are merely standing in for him. He is said to be embodied in a prominent pine tree at the top of the hill. Other tales say he returned in apparition form and told a friend he would appear at his

Doon Hill, at Aberfoyle, whose highest tree is reputed to contain the body of the Rev Robert Kirk, after he was spirited away by faeries

child's baptism. If the friend threw a knife over his head, he would be returned to the human world – but, alas, this did not happen. (Faeries were believed to not like iron, a belief which may arise from the fact that 'faeries' possibly had their origins in folktales about pre-Iron Age peoples.)

Mr Kirk's book has attracted folklorists from many countries, and specific attention from writers such as Sir Walter Scott, Robert Bontine Cunninghame Graham and Andrew Lang. He describes the faeries' social organisation, their habits, dwellings, food, crafts, talents, faults and sexual mores. As a seventh son, he was credited with the gift of healing and possibly of second sight. He placed the faeries between human beings and angels and interviewed people who claimed to have seen them or had their lives influenced by them.

Mr Kirk sincerely believed in these beings and his researches were, in his own mind, devoted to the study of real beings and not to stories or fables. Such beliefs in past centuries were strong and vibrant, and today it is still a fascinating subject.

THE DUKE'S PASS

THE DUKE'S PASS links Aberfoyle with the Loch Katrine road junction and Loch Achray. It is only four and a half miles (7km) long, but it is rich in evocative scenery, most notably containing three of the natural elements that characterise so much of the land in the Trossachs area. First is the white-barked birch tree with its lovely fronds – these trees once covered much of the Highland area, though now they have too often been replaced by modern conifers. It is technically classified as a weed, yet its soft wood was used for many purposes long ago and it is undeniably beautiful. It deserves to be cherished. Second is rock, the prominence of grey boulders and stone-studded little knolls or bluffs giving a sense of great antiquity. People long ago had a near-spiritual affinity with rock and it was not unknown for them to place their hands on a rock surface and stand and listen as if to internal vibes. Third is heather, the very essence of the public image of Scotland at the tail end of summer and early autumn. There is a great deal of this attractive purple plant along the sides of the Duke's Pass and long ago heather strands were used for bedding, ropes, thatch, brushes and dye for tartans and to make heather ale; it is also an important source of nectar for bees. Heather is the plant badge (or talisman) of Clan Donald and some other families.

Walkers enjoy themselves dancing around the Rev Robert Kirk's pine tree

To drive the Duke's Pass is to experience the true flavour of the Highlands. The landscape has changed as a result of so much conifer forestry, but it is still possible to sense the past. In my experience the route is best driven from south to north, first because the zig-zag pull up from Aberfoyle gives a strong sense of leaving the Lowlands, and also because from the crest of the pass there is a magnificent view to the nearby mountains and over miles of moorland. The Duke of Montrose, the landowner last century, built the first proper road, first to help cater for the massive influx of visitors following Sir Walter Scott's poem *The Lady of the Lake*, and also to get more easily from one end of his lands to the other. The road had a commercial character, too, because the bark of oak trees was used in the tanning of leather and charcoal was made which was used in iron smelting and the production of gunpowder. Oak woodland was 'managed' by coppice rotations. This crossing was, of course, used by earlier travellers, though they tended to take a lower line. Carriages found it hard and in its early days it was often little more than a bridle track for horses, though as time passed it improved. The steep gradients and tight bends that we know today date from 1932.

The road rises steeply from Aberfoyle, passing the entrance to the David Marshall Lodge or Queen Elizabeth Forest Park visitor centre. On the other side of the road the remnants of a huge slate quarry can be seen. Look at it from on the road, because the heaped-up piles are insecure, particularly after rain or melting ice. The blue slate roofed many houses in the area, and the quarry operated for over a century and produced over a million slates a year. It was second only to Ballachulish, near Glen Coe, in importance. At one time it employed over a hundred men, and they all lived in a now gone village. One (renovated) house remains.

Tartan-clad pipers can sometimes be seen and heard at the roadside. They are sometimes travelling people, who for a fee will pose with tourists. These people have a long pedigree. They are not gypsies although gypsies did (and do) come to Scotland, but they share the same form of nomadic living. Some are very wealthy and possess modern and well appointed caravans; others find life hard and still use gelly tents, comprising an old tarpaulin heaped over a framework of branches. Gelly derives from the Gaelic for 'shelter'. Some Highland travellers (tinkers is not a term favoured by them as a description) speak Gaelic, and they also have their own language called Cant. (My wife was a teacher to the travelling children; she drove a mobile school, and she still keeps up her contacts with the families.) Their origins are shadowy, but are linked to special crafts and skills like the making of jewellery or precious objects in silver and gold. At one time they had high caste status.

As the centuries passed, the travellers stayed on the road and their trades spread into making kitchen objects of tin (hence tinker) and working on the farms. They were joined by the victims of power struggles, people who had lost their lands and were known as 'broken men'. Others were victims of the Highland Clearances, evicted from ancestral lands to make

Opposite: The brown peat waters of a quiet burn run near an abandoned slate quarry on the Duke's Pass, not far from Aberfoyle

A piper in full Highland dress performs for visitors to the Duke's Pass

63

way for sheep or the creation of sporting estates. The MacPhees, for example, lost their lands on the west coast islands of Colonsay and Oronsay to the expansionist MacDonalds; they also lost parts of Lochaber, in the central Highlands, where they were part of Clan Cameron's contingents in the failed 1745 Jacobite Rising. Nowadays the travellers do a variety of tasks, such as making baskets, and selling white heather or scrap metal. However, many of their old camp sites are closed to them. Farming practices have changed, and this long-standing way of life is now threatened. But travelling is in their blood and not easily quenched.

The road passes the entrance to Forest Enterprise's car drive route in the Loch Achray Forest. It also passes below another knoll with an ancient name, Craig Vad, the 'crag of the wolf'. One of the reasons for the proliferation of red deer in modern times, and the subsequent damage to trees, is that the extinction of the wolf meant that the deer had no natural predator (other than man). There is much disputing as to when the last wolf was killed in Scotland and no area can be entirely sure that their claim is unique, but the late 1700s is the most likely time. Men who went from this area to the 1745 Rising had probably heard the wolf howl in Scotland (and their parents certainly had), but depending on the area, many had not seen a rabbit.

A sign of changing times is tiny Lochan Reoichte (pronounced 'roach'), meaning the 'frozen' or 'icy small loch', which lies just within the start of the Loch Achray forest drive. It was much loved by that great writer, traveller, politician and champion of causes, R.B. Cunninghame Graham (see p76, Lake of Menteith section). He wrote about it in his *Notes On The District Of Menteith* and for desolate beauty he placed it first amongst the hill lochans of the area. Nowadays it can be busy with people, but it is still beautiful. The visitor gets a clear view of the slate quarry across the road when at the side of this lochan. Just above the quarry are some cairns which, according to local tradition, mark a clash between cattle raiders from Lochaber who were chased by men from Menteith and Lennox and were killed on that spot. Cattle raiding long ago was considered more a manly sport than a crime, but even so, clashes could lead to full-blooded fights.

The traveller also gets a glimpse of what looks like a small loch buried in the trees on lower ground to the east of the

Lochan Reoichte is an early gem when driving or cycling on the Achray Forest Drive, in the Queen Elizabeth Forest Park

road: this is Loch Drunkie, which was once visited by Queen Victoria. It is larger than in past times as a result of water schemes. The forest drive and a pleasant walk pass its fringes. The name probably derives from the Gaelic *dronn*, meaning a 'ridge' or 'knoll', and *laidh* (locative ending) which may mean a place where there are ridges.

A viewpoint knoll on the west side of the Duke's Pass road and near the crest gives wide views, and there is now a small, walled enclosure and an indicator cairn there. In Gaelic it is called *Tom an t-Seallaidh*, literally 'the viewpoint knoll'. It is easy to imagine travellers in the past stopping here and looking over the wide sweep of woods, mountains and lochs. Although the spreading patchwork of modern forestry plantations is clear evidence of landscape which has changed, there is still something about this view which speaks of the past. There is a sense of how early travellers might have seen the Trossachs area, hill-shrouded with far-off lochs and a great deal of woodland. If it were a film of the American West it would be termed 'Injun territory' or 'badlands'.

The houses of modern Callander can be picked out, and the shining waters of Loch Venachar. Ben Ledi, the Beltane mountain, presents a broad flank and there is a long view to the houses of Brig o' Turk village and the open mouth and length of Glen Finglas, with the sheltering hill of Meal Cala at the back. The former Trossachs Hotel baronial towers catch the eye

A hillwalker on the summit of Ben A'n enjoys the view of Loch Katrine stretching out in the distance

Ben Venue, in the heart of the Trossachs, dominates the view from a knoll close to the Duke's Pass Road

(now a holiday complex), and alongside it is the pointed peak of 1,520ft (454m) Ben A'n. This hill is a favourite with rock climbers, but the non-rock walker can ascend it by a steep path which runs round the side of the cliff-section of the hill and takes the walker to the summit, thus avoiding the bluffs. Some hill walkers park themselves at the bottom of the crags and watch the rock climbers. Ben A'n has an intricate series of shortish climbs and dries quickly after rain.

The summit itself is a large rock which can only take a couple of people on top, but just beside it there is a grass section where visitors can sit comfortably and look down the length of Loch Katrine. Most of the loch can be seen, with the exception of the arm of Glen Gyle, where Rob Roy was born. It is truly a wonderful viewpoint and worth the slog. Sir Walter

Scott is to blame for calling this peak Ben A'n. It is actually Am Binnean, the Pinnacle, a name it deserves.

The visitor on *Tom an t-Seallaidh* also gets a glimpse of Loch Katrine and a good view of Ben Venue, which at 2,393 feet (729m) falls short of the 3,000ft Munro mountain level. There are arguments over this name: 'Mountain of the caves', 'of the young cattle' or 'of milk' have all been suggested, the last probably deriving from the white burns which lace its sides after heavy rain or melting snow. Ben Venue overlooks the historic Bealach nam Bo, the 'Pass of the Cattle', and cradles the Goblins' Corrie, both of which are dealt with in the section on Loch Katrine. There is an excellent view of the Bealach nam Bo and the Goblins' Corrie from the top of Ben A'n. Ben Venue is normally climbed from Loch Achray-side and by way of Gleann Riabhach or from Ledard, on the road from Aberfoyle to Inversnaid – but beware: despite large sums spent on renovation and repair, the paths are often eroded and boggy in the early sections, particularly after prolonged rain.

The Duke's Pass road is not long, but it is packed with historical interest. In time it leads to a westwards-running spur which ends at Loch Katrine, a name woven deep into the tapestry of the Trossachs.

FOREST PARK

IT IS DIFFICULT to escape the trees – and who would want to? The land was once largely covered with birch, rowan, oak, alder, hazel and pine and large areas were cleared for grazing, or the wood used as fuel, or to provide timber or to flush out 'broken men', fugitives from power struggles and persecution. Nowadays the tree is back, but this time in extensive commercial plantations, grown and harvested like any other crop, but thanks to some enlightened modern planting of different tree species, these forests produce a mosaic of colour across our landscape, particularly in autumn. They also provide local jobs and because the Forestry Commission is empowered by law to pay attention to leisure activity, the woods of the Queen Elizabeth Forest Park are managed in such a way that cycling on broad forestry tracks or walking on smaller paths can take place alongside forestry felling and other work.

It must be said clearly that the Commission has done an immense amount to improve the economic health of the area covered in this book. As the years have passed, some earlier errors in planting without sufficient regard for 'look' have been corrected, and much of the woodland is now a rich habitat for a wide variety of birds and animals and particularly capercaillie, black grouse and red squirrels, and this is a joy to the visitor's eye. Native Scots pine are being planted to help with this aspect of conservation. One visitor said the park's outline looks like a hand held up with the thumb extended, a well known sign of cheer or jubilation, and that is

Top: This attractive sign at the Queen Elizabeth Forest Park visitor centre outlines some of the main themes: forests, hills and wildlife
Above: A wood carver displays his skills inside the centre

appropriate because the park is an essential part of the tourism format of Loch Lomond, the Trossachs and the Rob Roy country.

The park runs from the east shore of Loch Lomond to a point close to the village of Thornhill, also to north of Aberfoyle and over towards Callander, then the thumb points north to cover Strathyre; in all it is over 50,000 acres (20,000 hectares), straddling the boundary between Highland and Lowland. The Commission's public-action arm, Forest Enterprise, does much to deepen the enjoyment of visitors. The park was named after the present queen, and therein lies an interesting and sensitive historical point: note that no numeral is used. It is not the Queen Elizabeth 11 Forest Park and the reason for this is that Queen Elizabeth 1 was queen of England, but not of Scotland, because at that time Scotland was an independent nation. When the present queen came to the throne some organisations, including the Post Office, began to use the insignia E 11 R in Scotland, and some Scots objected on the grounds of historical accuracy (the Union of the Crowns between Scotland and England, when James VI became James 1 of England, took place in 1603). There was quite a lot of public feeling on this issue and some E 11 R signs were torn down or, in the case of an Edinburgh pillar box, dynamited. Common sense prevailed – it is a matter of historical accuracy – and the Forestry Commission had the good sense to use Queen Elizabeth without the offending numeral.

Extensive tracts of woodland catch the visitor's eye – oak, birch,

Modern forestry has changed the Highland landscape. Trees now cover the hills at Strathyre, not far from Balquhidder and Loch Earn

Forests are harvested in the same manner as other crops. These logs await collection in the Strathyre Forest

Norway spruce, Sitka spruce, silver firs, larch and rowan, often an oasis of colour created by the forester's planting designs and by storms. The Commission owned woodland here as early as the 1930s and the foresters over the years have included men made redundant from the old slate quarry on the Duke's Pass road, women workers during World War II when most of the men were serving in the Forces, prisoners of war and displaced persons. Even Sir Walter Scott was involved in a tree-felling row in past times: this arose when some woods on the shoulders of Ben Venue which were owned by the Duke of Montrose were about to be cut down. Scott, who loved the Trossachs, was distressed and a public outcry arose. Scott wanted to raise the purchase price by penny subscription – but, alas, the woods were cut down, despite their petitioning.

Miles of the modern forest 'roads' are used for walking, cycling and car rallies and if you see some husky dogs there in the winter, don't think you have made a serious navigational error because husky dog racing with sleds goes on there as well. The park was given its name in celebration of the coronation of the Queen in 1953. Cars belonging to the public are not allowed on the forest roads – with one exception: a forest drive in the Loch Achray forest was opened in 1977 to celebrate the silver jubilee of the Queen.

Just above Aberfoyle and a key part of the park lies a prominent visitor centre: its 'proper' name is the David Marshall Lodge, although the tag 'Forest Park visitor centre' is used more and more by the public. It is owned and managed by the Commission, who received it from the Carnegie Trust in 1960. The Trust had a policy of naming projects after their chairman in the given year, hence David Marshall. The centre has displays about forestry operations and the geology and history of the area and altogether does an excellent educational job. It has marvellous views in all directions, to the Campsies and the fort-hill of Dumgoyne, to the Fintry hills, to the low-lying ground of farms and mosses, to the close-up Menteith hills, to Ben Lomond. Nearby Lime Craig has spectacular views to the bigger hills of the north, and the forests surrounding the centre have educative trails, including two waterfalls and the Highland Boundary Fault. Ben Lomond itself was sold by the Commission to the National Trust for Scotland in 1985.

The visitor centre's opening times are seasonal. The Commission also operates two camp and caravan sites, on the banks of Loch Lomond at Cashel, and at Cobleland, in the Trossachs, near Aberfoyle. There is also a log cabin site on the shores of Loch Lubnaig, between Callander and Strathyre.

A large part of the long-distance footpath, the West Highland Way, runs through the forest park on Loch Lomond-side and there are oak woods at Rowardennan; these are specially protected. Charcoal was obtained there from timber and used in iron smelting and the bark of trees was used in the tanning of leather. The oak woods of Ptarmigan, Ross Wood, Sallochy and Blair Wood are a forest nature reserve within the park. Many trees in past times were cleared for homesteads and the woods contain old settlements, the faint, moss-covered outlines of dwellings, including some of the homes of the McGregors. These oak woods were bought from the Montrose Estates by the Commission in 1951. Forest Enterprise plan to convert all of their conifer forests on the east shore of Loch Lomond to native oak, birch, ash, rowan, holly and Scots pine, which is a mammoth project.

When admiring the shape and colours of much of the modern forestry planting, it is fitting to remember Alistair Cameron, the first Head Forester of the Strathyre planting in the 1930s and 1940s. When clear felling took place, the Commission drew up landscape plans for the forests to the west of Loch Lubnaig and to the north and east of Strathyre village; these were done with an eye for look, as well as tackling practical commercial points. There is a Cameron's Viewpoint in the woods there. As already mentioned, now that the wolf has gone, the red deer have no natural predator and they can destroy many young trees. To protect them, many plantations have to be fenced off and deer culls put into operation.

In some ways the wheel has gone full circle: the old woods were cleared, a cattle economy was operated, more felling went on, in came the sheep and the sporting estates and now the woodlands are being restored.

The delicate beauty of cones on a spruce tree. The new forests already contain an abundance of plant and wildlife

This farm near the exit of the Achray Forest Drive occupies an ancient site and incorporates old and modern buildings

Foresters would be the first to say that all is not perfect and that mistakes were made in past times, but the modern forester strives to plant with functional skill and yet to present an attractive landscape, with natural clumps left unfelled, by mixing species, by providing plantations with curved edges or with boundaries of deciduous trees, with gaps alongside the courses of burns or the banks of lochs. The result today is a richness which makes this old landscape live again.

The folklore of trees is also absorbing. People long ago believed that trees often contained good and bad spirits, hence the flowers, plants and leaves badges of the clans. These were not for identification, as is often said, but were talismans and charms. For instance, the rowan or mountain ash was widely believed to provide protection against evil. Most houses had one planted outside and rowans were cherished. In modern times there is a tale of a forester having to cut down a large rowan and his colleagues jokingly advising him against it. But he cut it down anyway... and it then fell across his cab.

And what happens to the timber? Sawlogs are produced from the bottom end of the trunks and are sawn into planks for timber which is used in house construction, fences, gates and packaging. Sawdust and the edges of logs are sold to the chipboard mills who also use roundwood, the forester's name for smaller trees and the tops of larger ones, and produce material for building and the furniture industry. The paper mills are the major users of roundwood.

'Jock, when ye hae naething else to do, ye may be aye sticking in a tree; it will be growing, Jock, when ye're sleeping.'

(*The Laird of Dumbiedyke's advice to his son in Sir Walter Scott's novel* The Heart of Midlothian, *part of which is the motto of the Royal Scottish Forestry Society.*)

THE LAKE OF MENTEITH

SOME HISTORICAL SITES are unforgettable for all the right reasons, and the Lake of Menteith and the small wooded island of Inchmahome are in that category. The wide loch stretches out in the boundary land between Highland and Lowland, flanked on one side by the steep-sided Menteith hills and on the others fringed by woodland which in certain lights can sometimes have the malevolent look of the Wild Wood in Edinburgh-born Kenneth Grahame's famous book for children (and which is really for adults), *The Wind in the Willows.* Beyond this woodland lie modern farms, perched on grassy slopes or standing on ground reclaimed from the great chain of bogs and marshes which in past times made much of this land impassable. This bogland, the remnants of which are now of special environmental interest, is popularly known as the Flanders Moss, but it is split up into different bog or former bog areas with separate names. It is sometimes said that the name 'Flanders' comes from Belgium, the Netherlands and France, because dried moss was used as padding for bandages in World War I, but the name is older and is probably a corruption of a Scots word, flinders, meaning 'to shake' or 'to tremble'. The cattle drovers and warring armies knew they could cross the infant River Forth at a place called the Fords of Frew, but other than that the bogland in past centuries blocked the movement of wagons, cavalry and herds and emphasised the strategic importance of royal Stirling and its famous bridge.

It is frequently and erroneously said that the Lake of Menteith is Scotland's only lake and that it was given an Anglicised name because one of the Stewarts of Menteith allegedly betrayed the Scottish patriot and Guardian of Scotland, Sir William Wallace, to the invading English. All this is bunkum, however, and there are several lochs in Scotland called 'lake'. The Lake of Menteith was formerly called 'loch' and the name switch was made by map makers last century who probably did not mean any harm by it. In spring and summer the woods, shores, the three islands and the

shimmering waters can be breathtakingly beautiful, and indeed the same is true of autumn when the leaves change to gold and red. The rowing boats of anglers dot the loch in season, co-existing with herons, swans and great crested grebes. In severe winters the loch freezes and in modern times it has been possible to walk over to the islands; people skate and slide and some hardy souls have taken cars onto the ice. Curling matches – a kind of winter bowls, but with sliding 'stones' instead of balls – are held in the old style. One of the most historic curling matches, the Grand Match between the north and south of Scotland, was last held there in 1979.

The island of Inchmahome – meaning 'island of St Colm' – is in the care of the government department, Historic Scotland. They operate a ferry service in season from the handful of houses, the church and hotel that make up the Port of Menteith. The island has the grey ruins of a priory on it and it was visited by King Robert the Bruce during the Scottish Wars of Independence and also by the youthful Mary Queen of Scots who was sent there for safety when she was a child. Henry VIII of England wanted to marry her to his son, Edward, but the Scots did not want this marriage. In 1547 an English army invaded the Borders and ranged here and there, burning and pillaging, in an attempt to coerce the Scots into agreeing. This episode is known to historians as the 'Rough Wooing'. Even the massive castle at Stirling was not considered safe, so Mary was taken by her mother, the redoubtable Mary of Guise, to Inchmahome for three weeks, where it was considered she could not readily be taken by surprise, and could more easily be taken into Highland fastnesses if need be. There can be poignant moments when on Inchmahome, with the wind in the trees, the soft lapping of the waters of the loch, and the memories of the singing of the Augustinian monks who built the priory and of the small girl who despite being made to do her lessons and help with gardening, must have wearied of the confines of the island and wondered what on earth would happen to her.

The great Walter Comyn, Earl of Menteith, brought the monks to the island in about 1238. Establishing a religious colony in this way was something powerful magnates did at that time. It was considered to be a pious deed with an element of spiritual protection for the men and women who acted in this way, besides a considerable sum of money about it. There was a church of a kind on Inchmahome before the priory was built and the Menteith earls had a house on a neighbouring island, Inch Talla.

The monks were known as canons and spent their days in prayer and contemplation, study and worship, tending their gardens and catching fish. They followed the canon, or Rule, for monastic communities inspired by St Augustine of Hippo (354–430) who founded their order. The prior was often one of the leading men of the time who sometimes played an active part in the life of the nation – no easy matter, with Scotland being invaded by English monarchs. As the centuries passed the spiritual health of the priory declined and by the later Middle Ages a pat-

Opposite: Charming Port of Menteith is the departure point for Historic Scotland's ferry to Inchmahome, on the Lake of Menteith

Historic Scotland's notice tells visitors how to summon the ferry to Inchmahome

tern had developed of monarchs appointing commendators as heads of abbeys and priories. These were often uncaring and even immoral men who saw the religious establishments as easy pickings for wealth. The priory declined further at the Reformation. It came into the hands of the Erskine family and then the Grahams of Montrose, until finally the State took care of it in 1926.

Today the buildings are mainly roofless and the walls are shells, but there is still a lot to see of an establishment which must have caused gasps in its day. The nearby trees and Historic Scotland's practice of cropping the grass close all around enhance the ancient ruins. The choir section has wall plaques and grave slabs to the Graham family, including the valiant

The grave of 'Don Roberto',
R.B. Cunninghame Graham, at
Inchmahome

R.B. Cunninghame Graham, writer, traveller, politician and a descendant of kings, a man who was a champion of the poor and an enemy of injustice. He was a co-founder of the Scottish Labour Party in the 1880s and in 1928 the first president of the Scottish National Party. He was known as 'Don Roberto' because of his travels in Latin America and he is still honoured in Paraguay and Argentina in particular. He was jailed for taking part in an alleged illegal assembly in Trafalgar Square, London, called to discuss unemployment and the (then) Irish question: he was also the Queen's deputy lieutenant of the county of Stirling and he distributed as his official photograph a shot of himself in prison garb. He loved horses and the brand he used to identify them can be seen on his gravestone. His wife, generally known as Gabrielle de la Balmondiere, is buried alongside him. She has been described variously as an orphan, a gamin and a Chilean princess, but she was actually Caroline Horsfall, an actress and dancer, the runaway daughter of a Yorkshire surgeon. She was a pioneer of women's rights, an historian and writer, and a sterling character. Don Roberto was once the best known Scot of his time; for a while his star waned, though happily in our present age it is rising again.

The chapter house – so called because the monastic community met there daily and a chapter of their Rule was read before meetings – contains one of the most moving stone effigies in Scotland: it is of Walter, the first earl of the Stewart line who died around 1295, and his countess Mary, their little dogs lying at their feet. She has her arm around him, and theirs is a love story told again and again over the centuries. Also in the chapter house is an upright fourteenth-century slab with a carving of Sir John Drummond with spear and shield; the Drummonds were a family who aided the priory.

Some of the stone carvings show a design depicting a series of squares known as 'the checky'; in past centuries this was a method of keeping financial accounts. It was taken into the heraldic coat of arms of the Stewarts when they became High Stewards of Scotland and it also appears

The ancient ruins of Inchmahome Priory, founded by Walter Comyn, Earl of Menteith, around 1238. Mary Queen of Scots took refuge with the Augustinian monks at the priory when she was a small girl

on the hats of Scottish police officers where it signifies guardianship and protection. It gave us the words 'cheque' and 'exchequer'.

Some places bear visiting again and again and Inchmahome is one such place. Historic Scotland have a small shop/office and discreet toilets on the island, but because it is a sacred place and burial ground it is managed with sensitivity. Visitors are asked to behave sensibly and to take all litter home.

Inchmahome is a place where hard-eyed fighting men discussed the great affairs of State, where the cowled canons sang and worked, where a small girl and her mother looked anxiously at any boat coming towards the island and where Don Roberto, who knew and loved the great pampas of parts of South America, could also delight in this land of wood, mountain and water.

It is truly a jewel in the crown of this part of Scotland.

7 Heading Westwards:
Redcoats and Clanspeople

THE ROAD FROM THE FORESTRY VILLAGE of Aberfoyle runs westwards for 15 miles (24km) until it ends at the small harbour and large hotel at Inversnaid on the east shore of Loch Lomond. It is truly one of the most scenic routes in the country, but it needs responsible driving; in fact, it's not a bad idea to swap drivers every now and again so that everyone gets a chance to wonder at the stunning views of the lochs, hills and woods, as well as having to concentrate on staying on the tarmac. Veteran writer, novelist and historian Nigel Tranter called this road 'one of the most delightful stretches of road in mid-Scotland' and said it featured 'some of the finest scenery in the south Highlands'. He also campaigned to have its surface improved.

Opposite: Tourist boats in the harbour at Inversnaid on the east shore of Loch Lomond

'Travelling westwards' is an evocative phrase and it lodged in the mind of the poet William Wordsworth when he and his sister Dorothy had occasion to be at a ferryman's hut on the shores of Loch Katrine on 11 September 1803: it was a Sunday and a quiet, sweet evening with a glow in the west, and here they met two Highland women, hatless but neatly dressed. The two ladies greeted the Wordsworths and after a few minutes' conversation one of them said: 'What? Are you stepping westwards?' This exchange made a deep impression on William and he later wrote a poem which he called *Stepping Westwards*. In fact the Wordsworths so liked the scenery between Loch Katrine and Loch Lomond that they made this journey three times.

In past years people could sail up Loch Katrine from the Trossachs pier to Stronachlachar at the west end of the loch and then take a pony over the remaining distance to Inversnaid. Nowadays the whole journey can be done by car and coach on the modern B829 and the linking minor road. A spur runs down to Stronachlachar where passengers can still alight from the steamer which sails from the Trossachs pier. This road has single-track sections with passing places, blind bends and braes, and recent renovation has left a high boundary edge like the side of a table, which can spell disaster if a car dips a wheel. Major hold-ups used to be caused when modern coaches met head on, but mobile phones have helped in this respect because coach drivers leaving Aberfoyle or Inversnaid can now stagger their runs to avoid meeting on awkward sections. Patient, careful driving and a sense of humour will generally overcome most problems encountered on this road. Don't hesitate to use

*Creag More, once a MacGregors'
sentinel hill, overlooks Aberfoyle*

your horn on blind bends or summits, and do keep your speed down.

This is an ancient route and where modern vehicles now run, the cattle drovers once made their way from the west to the huge markets at Crieff and Falkirk. The Hanoverian military road builders toiled here, with a constant wary eye on the hostile MacGregors who frequently attacked them. As the driver leaves Aberfoyle the eastern part of three miles long (5km) Loch Ard fringes the road, with exquisite views to Ben Lomond; these figure in some renowned 1924 etchings by artist D.Y. Cameron. This is the Pass of Aberfoyle, part of long Strath Ard, and Scott brought a lot of this scenery into his novels *Rob Roy* and *Waverley*. It was mainly MacGregor country long ago, a clan held in great affection by Scott.

Loch Ard's banks have greatly changed in modern times, largely because of the extensive planting of conifer forest. It was once a botanists' paradise. The name is sometimes given as 'the high loch', but 'loch of the height' might be more appropriate because the scenery becomes increasingly stern; the rocky bluffs include an Echo Rock. Queen Victoria liked it and wrote in her diaries: 'Certainly one of the loveliest drives I can remember, along Loch Ard, a fine, long loch with trees of all kinds overhanging the road, heather making all pink, bracken, rocks, high hills of such shape, and trees growing up them as in Switzerland.'

This loch and its shores and islands were a bolt-hole and hunting base for the powerful Murdoch Stewart, Regent of Scotland, Duke of Albany and Earl of Fife when James I of Scotland was a prisoner in England. Duke Murdoch was executed in Stirling for treason in 1423 because the returning king felt he had been less than enthusiastic about getting the king back and had upwardly mobile ideas of his own. Other members of his family, including his sons, Walter and Alexander, were also executed and with great ferocity, as was the Earl of Lennox. Some historians have speculated that the king concocted charges and got rid of possible rivals before they could organise a coup against him.

Former shooting lodges such as Altskeith and Foresthills alongside the Loch Ard section of the road are now attractive hotels or time-share buildings. The road also passes the nineteenth-century farm of Ledard where the burn has a fine waterfall, and where a well-used path leads up the glen to Ben Bhreac ('the dappled mountain') and on to Ben Venue. Scott was much impressed by the waterfall and brought it and this glen into both *Rob Roy* and *Waverley* (a story of the 1745 Jacobite Rising). Visitors to Scotland should note that Scott's fame and prowess as an historical novelist and his Waverley Novels are commemorated in the name of Edinburgh's main rail station. Kinlochard – the head of the loch – is a surprisingly large and scattered group of houses, with several homes tucked away in the trees. There is a shop and a sailing club. The old Mill of Chon stands on its fringes; like Aberfoyle, it is basically a forestry village.

The traveller proceeding westwards should look out for a house on the right-hand side of the road. It is sited near a small hump-backed bridge and has what looks like a sheep pen at the side. This 'pen' is the remains of an inn called The Teapot, where travellers of yesteryear could get something which looked like tea, but certainly wasn't. Illicit whisky-making was regarded as a normal pursuit by most Highlanders and whisky jars were hidden at the side of this burn. It must have been potent stuff because evidently a fiddler fell off this bridge during a wedding and was killed. In 1832 alone there were 14,000 prosecutions for illegally distilling whisky and the following year a rapacious government made the landowner liable for any stills found. As a result of this, owners cracked down on their own folk, though often reluctantly.

Gold was also mined in this corner for a time last century, but without commercial success.

The road passes through some beautiful deciduous woodland as well as conifer plantations; in these woods can be found the ruins and gable ends of houses which once formed part of MacGregor townships. A private road leads to Comer Farm at the 'back' of Ben Lomond, once home to Rob Roy MacGregor's wife, Mary. The road runs closely along the side of another beautiful tree-shrouded loch, Loch Chon (pronounced 'hon'), meaning 'loch of the dogs' and which takes its name from an island used as a kennels for hunting dogs. Loch Chon has parking bays and picnic places, and in the summer season is alive with the laughter of children, and yet it still has a fey

The narrow isthmus at Tarbet, between Loch Long and Loch Lomond, has pleasant forest walks

feeling. Tradition says that it has a supernatural water dog; other sources say the mysterious being is a water bull.

Above the loch is Coir-Shian', cave (or corrie) of the 'Men of Peace', which can be another name for faeries. People avoided a series of small hills here after sunset because they were believed to be faery knolls. It was thought that on Hallow Eve, any person going round one of these hills nine times to the left, would find a door opening which would beckon them inside the hill.

The westwards scenery now changes to open moorland and hill and the B829 divides into two minor roads: the eastern one runs half a mile down to Stronachlachar on the south-west side of Loch Katrine, where the public road ends. The westwards arm runs along the north shore of Loch Arklet and ends at Inversnaid. Loch Arklet used to drain into Loch Lomond, but as part of the water scheme it was raised to three times its former level and is now linked to Loch Katrine. The name 'Arklet' is a puzzle; one source suggests that it means 'of the snowflakes', which may refer to its original size and appearance in certain lights. We owe a lot to Dorothy Wordsworth for detailed descriptions of Highland life last century, and she found the original Loch Arklet-side well inhabited (now it has one farm). She admired hay patches and people at work and the bright flowers of potato plants.

On the north side of the road is a large farm, Corriearklet, and according to the register of Buchanan parish, Rob Roy and Mary were married on this site at New Year in 1693. At that time a group of about twenty houses formed a township here. By a law of 1690 all weddings had to be in church, but many Highlanders, and particularly their leaders, refused to do this. The church buildings were often dirty and even Sunday services were commonly held outside in the kirkyard if the weather permitted. Ministers connived at weddings being held in houses and barns: the groom paid a small fine and the wedding was held in the bride's house or that of a relative. Festivities could go on for days and included competitions involving weapons such as bows and muskets and Highland games and trials of strength.

As the modern traveller continues westwards the peaks of the mountains known as the Arrochar Alps come prominently into view. Arrochar is a village at the north end of tidal Loch Long and linked to Loch Lomond by the Tarbet isthmus. Loch Arklet and Loch Lomond are only about a mile apart, but Loch Arklet is 500ft (150m) higher, and these peaks don't appear at first sight to be to the west of Loch Lomond. They are all striking mountains, the most prominent being Ben Ime (3,318ft/1,011m), 'the butter mountain' (it had sheiling areas at its foot); flat-topped Ben Narnain (3,036ft/926m), whose name is obscure, and its spur, A'Chrois (The Cross); Ben Vane (3,004ft/915m), 'the middle mountain'; and Ben Vorlich (3,092ft/931m), 'mountain of the sea bag' (bay), a name sometimes used when a loch looks like a sea-loch. It is interesting that there is another Ben Vorlich at Loch Earn, and the loch has the same bay-like appearance. Ben

Tarbet with the peak of Ben Lomond in the background

The east shore of Loch Lomond, north of Inversnaid, contains a cave-refuge used by Rob Roy

Rob Roy's viewpoint near Inversnaid looks over ground once controlled by the Highland hero

Vane and Ben Vorlich cradle the higher and hidden Loch Sloy, 'loch of the hosts', whose name is the war slogan of the Clan MacFarlane, and whose waters are now part of a huge series of hydro-electric loch-dams and pipes, many constructed in the period following World War II. The work was often done by armies of navvies (as was the earlier Loch Katrine scheme), including many men from Ireland. Huge pipes coming out of the sides of Ben Vorlich are a major engineering feat, but they are also a scenic blemish. Nowadays public opinion is far more aware of such issues and if this scheme were constructed today, these pipes would be put underground and certainly now that Loch Lomond has been selected for National Park status.

The MacFarlanes were great cattle raiders. It is said that they paid for their daughters (*tochers*) by the light of the Michelmas moon: in other words, when the autumn moons came (like the Commanche moon of the old American West) they set out to steal other people's cattle to pay for their daughters' dowries. At that point in the year the moon gave enough light for raiding, but not too much to prevent concealment. Furthermore, cattle at the tail end of summer were in good condition.

The MacFarlanes had a castle on a small island in Inveruglas bay, just across Loch Lomond from Inversnaid. Just before the westwards road drops down to Inversnaid and the waters of Loch Lomond, a white farm and small school can be seen on the north side of the road, with a very evocative and historical name: Garrison. The ruins of a Hanoverian fort and a graveyard for soldiers and their womenfolk stand here, a relic of times when Redcoat troops endeavoured to patrol these MacGregor-owned lands. Rob Roy himself had a house on the side of the Snaid burn, but further up the glen. The fort was built by the Duke of Montrose after the 1715 Jacobite Rising and – of all things – on land seized from Rob Roy. Twice the MacGregors attacked it and burned it down. When the 1745 Rising came along, twelve MacGregors captured the garrison of eighty-nine men. Most were out road-making and were taken by surprise.

After the Jacobite cause went down for ever at Culloden in 1746, the fort was repaired. General Wolfe, the victor of the key Quebec and Heights of Abraham battle against the French in Canada, served here for a time. He had no cause to love clansmen, but he respected their prowess as soldiers. The remains of the fort are now incorporated into a working farm and modern visitors should look at it from the road or from a viewpoint and indicator knoll on the south side of the road and named after Rob Roy. There is parking space here and a narrow bridge for cars across the foaming Snaid burn.

There are way-marked walks in the woods and a church stands close by, dedicated to St Kentigerna and now an outdoor centre. The church commemorates the MacGregors of Corriearklet, but Rob Roy was not married in any earlier church on this site, although that is often said. The name dedication to St Kentigerna is an historic one: she was an anchoress who died on Inch Cailleach (inch means 'an island') on Loch Lomond around 773. The ruins of a church can be seen there. She was of Irish royal blood, her father

The magical scenery of Loch Arklet with the 'Arrochar Alps' in the background

being Cellach, prince of Leinster. She married a neighbouring prince and had a son, Fillan. After her husband's death she left Ireland, lived as a nun in Scotland and eventually settled on Inch Cailleach (see Loch Lomond Islands).

The road now enters a new world, moving from the stark hillsides of Loch Arklet and plunging down through thick woodland to the bay of Inversnaid. Here there is ample parking space and the big Victorian hotel is both a memorial to the tourists of yesteryear who came by boat and horse-drawn coach and also testimony to the popularity of modern tourism. Cruising boats and a ferry run across Loch Lomond from the village of Inveruglas, Tarbet pier and other places to Inversnaid, and thousands of West Highland Way walkers make Inversnaid hotel a rest-place or have a meal and a drink before plodding off again.

There is no road on this gloriously wooded east side of Loch Lomond north of Rowardennan and short-stay visitors to Inversnaid often walk short distances up and down the West Highland Way path. This is particularly true of the northwards section where, just under a mile from Inversnaid and in a great huddle of boulders, Rob Roy had a reputed cave-refuge. There is a small direction sign on the path, but finding the cave is not easy and the rocks and steep path are difficult for those who are not nimble; in fact it is more of a fissure or a sheltered crack than a cave. With grotesque insensitivity the word 'cave' has been painted on the rocks at the side in letters big enough to be seen by boats on the loch. Dorothy Wordsworth visited the cave twice, once in 1803 with William and Coleridge, and once with a large party off a steamer, four years after Scott's *Rob Roy* was published.

The visitor can sometimes see goats on the paths, descendants of those kept by people – mainly MacGregors or their successors – who once lived on these hillsides and on the loch shore and which are now 'wild'. There is a strong tradition that King Robert the Bruce hid in a cave here when he was a fugitive during the Scottish Wars of Independence and some sources say it was the same one used later by Rob Roy. The story goes that some goats obligingly lay down at the entrance to the cave and so Bruce's pursuers thought it was empty and did not search it.

Good walking country... this restored church near Inversnaid is now an outdoor centre

Inversnaid is a beautiful corner, with the cradling woods, the little harbour and its pleasure craft, and a large waterfall – admittedly smaller than in past times because of the Loch Arklet changes, but still impressive after prolonged rain or melting snow. American writer Nathaniel Hawthorne came to Inversnaid in 1857 and thought that the scenery contained the most beautiful lake and mountain view he had ever seen. It can be startling to stand on the pier and look at the big hills and the long loch, and realise that Inversnaid is only 25 miles (40km) – as the crow flies – from Glasgow or Stirling. Consider, too, that the busy A82 main road from Glasgow to the north is less than a mile away by boat – but a 55-mile (88km) drive is needed to get over there.

The name 'Snaid' means 'a needle' (a reference to the burn), but 'a place where the woods have opened up' has also been suggested. This was very much Clan Gregor land. Rob Roy was laird of Craigroystan and Inversnaid and the remains of old houses can be seen in the woods and on the hillsides. These houses can seem small and primitive by modern standards, but they

The Inversnaid scenery inspired the writer Nathaniel Hawthorne

were snug and could be rebuilt fairly easily in times of strife. It has to be remembered that people lived elsewhere during the sheiling times and a 'big house' was not appropriate. It was generally a much healthier life than, say, an industrial slum in later times, or a cramped emigrant 'coffin ship'.

The Royal Society for the Protection of Birds has a well managed reserve on the north side of Inversnaid and a hillside path passes the ruins of old houses. There is also a particularly evocative group up the east side of the Snaid burn. By clan custom people were not permitted to marry until they had obtained land. The people who lived in these houses would have lived alongside their cattle, separated only by a wattle wall. They kept horses, hens and goats, and set up house by the old Highland pattern of begging, called *fraighdhe* in Gaelic and *thigging* in Lowland Scots. The groom-to-be would have moved around his friends and relatives and begged from each a cow or a sheep or seed to sow his land, or wood for his roof-tree; these were the predecessors of modern wedding presents.

Inversnaid is a place to linger and it has undoubtedly left its mark on both the literary and the conservation world. We have already mentioned at the beginning of this chapter that when the Wordsworths came here they met two Highland girls, the beauty, grace and courtesy of one in particular catching Dorothy's eye. As we have seen, she and William were given shelter, food and dry clothes in a ferryman's house (now replaced by the hotel). Dorothy wrote of people coming to church by boat from the other side of the loch, the men wearing tartan plaids and bonnets, and the women scarlet cloaks and green umbrellas; she noted how healthy the people were, with good looks and excellent teeth. William was so impressed that he wrote a poem, now known as 'The Highland Girl'. Its full title was in fact *To A Highland Girl At Inversnayde Upon Loch Lomond*:

> *Sweet Highland Girl, a very shower*
> *Of beauty is thy earthly dower!*

William's other famous poem often attributed to this area, *The Solitary Reaper*, was in fact inspired by a phrase in Thomas Wilkinson's *Tours of the British Mountains*, but he and Dorothy did in fact see the reapers when they crossed from Loch Katrine to Balquhidder.

The Jesuit poet, Gerard Manley Hopkins (1844–89), came to Inversnaid when he was working as a priest in a Glasgow parish. He had an intense sense of divine creation in nature and deplored the erosion of the countryside in the face of the expanding cities and towns of the Industrial Revolution. He admired the waterfall and the Snaid burn and the last verse of his sixteen-line poem *Inversnaid* is frequently quoted:

> *What would the world be, once bereft*
> *Of wet and of wildness? Let them be left,*
> *O let them be left, wildness and wet;*
> *Long live the weeds and the wilderness yet.*

Opposite: Inversnaid waterfall, on the east shore of Loch Lomond, helped inspire a famous poem

8 Loch Lomond: The Jewel Islands and the Wooded East

By yon bonnie banks and by yon bonnie braes,
Where the sun shines bright on Loch Lomond
Where me and my true love were ever wont to gae,
On the bonnie, bonnie banks of Loch Lomond.

SO RUNS THE FAMOUS SONG which makes Loch Lomond so well known. Furthermore, if a list were to be compiled of the world's best known one hundred songs, then *Loch Lomond* would probably be there, and amongst English-speaking nations it would most certainly be in the top quarter. It is one of the world's best known lakes and whilst the old tale behind the song might lack supportive evidence, it is a fitting anecdote. It suits the rippling waters, the wooded shores, the emerald islands, the glens which once knew Highland clanspeople, and with Ben Lomond's broad shoulders over all. It deserves to be true, this old tale of the Jacobite clansman being executed at Carlisle in the north of England, one of an abandoned garrison when Prince Charles Edward Stuart's army retreated north, never to return. His grief-stricken lover will take the high road back to Scotland by foot, and he will take the way of the spirit and the soul and he'll be in Scotland before her – though some versions of the song put it the other way round. The song recalls with nostalgia the steep sides of Ben Lomond, and the trees and birds, and lovers' trysts. Whatever its authenticity, it is a lovely song and deserves its popularity.

Loch Lomond is special, though some car-borne visitors wonder why as they speed up and down the busy A82 on the west side of the loch – and it is true that some sections of the mid-west or northern part, although still attractive, can look very similar to some other Scottish lochs. But Loch Lomond is really three lochs to me (others argue for two) because the fiord-like, narrow north end, the scattering of islands in the broad and shallow south corner, and the marshes and growing farmland of the area of the southern river, the Endrick Water, are all widely different in character. Put together, the loch is a place of mountains, moors, woods, beaches, islands, marshes

Ben Lomond's broad shoulders overlook the famous loch close to the village of Luss

and fields, with its top end in the Highlands and the southern end in the Lowlands.

Loch Lomond has many faces and some of them need caution. In bad weather it can be like the sea, with white-topped waves crashing on the shore, and in good weather it can be like paradise, with families splashing in the shallows and sun-worshipping on golden beaches. There is a nudist colony on the loch's biggest island, Inchmurrin, and they must know something about the midges the rest of us don't know! Loch Lomond has been compared to Loch Maree in Wester Ross, and there are certainly similarities, with Slioch peering down like Ben Lomond and several wooded islands, but there the similarity ends, because Loch Maree is lonely and Loch Lomond has the mark of people on its shores and islands.

It is only half an hour's drive from Scotland's biggest city of Glasgow to the town of Balloch at the loch's southern end. Generations of Glaswegians have found adventure, happiness and refreshment of spirit there. The railway came in 1850 and the first pleasure steamer, *The Marion*, was launched as early as 1832. Lochside communities were served by boat and thousands of visitors took to cruising. The big steamers have gone – hopefully, temporarily – but dozens of smaller pleasure and cruise ships and local ferries sail out from Balloch and the lochside villages and other sites, such as Luss, Inveruglas, Balmaha, Tarbet and Rowardennan. The steamer *The Maid of the Loch* is currently in dock at Balloch, and an appeal has been lodged to get her sailing again.

To experience Loch Lomond fully, a visitor has to sail around and through its mosaic of islands, and in doing so he or she is in the wake of many earlier peoples. One of the best outings is to go on the mailboat run to the inhabited islands. This operates from MacFarlane's boatyard at Balmaha on the eastern shore of the loch.

The early landscape was gouged out twice by ice and the movement of glaciers known as the Loch Lomond re-advance. The trough of the loch was pushed southwards right through the geological feature, the Highland Boundary Fault, where the old mountain mass of the Highlands came up against the younger and softer red sandstones of the lower ground. The line of the fault is clearly seen running from the River Fruin on the loch's west shore across the islands of Inchmurrin, Creeinch, Torrinch and Inchailloch, and up and over prominent Conic Hill on the east shore.

Loch Lomond is regarded by many people as the premier loch of Scotland. It is the largest body of inland water in the United Kingdom, covering over 27 square miles (70sq km). It is 23 miles (37km) long, the second longest to Loch Ness, and at 623ft (190m), the third deepest after Morar (1,017ft/310m) and Ness (754ft/230m). Before the thirteenth century it was known as Loch Leven or Levand from the vale and river of Leven, the only outlet from Balloch in the south to Dumbarton on the Clyde. The foot of the loch is only four miles (6km) from tidal waters, and the top end just under two miles (3km) from the sea loch of Loch Long at Arrochar.

It was a place for journeying long ago when the lochs and rivers were used as highways. The people of the dim centuries, the new Stone Age and Iron Age races, came here and left standing stones, hill forts, cup-and-ring marks and burial mounds on the loch shores and islands. The wandering people were succeeded by Neolithic farmers who left traces of houses, stockades and cultivation. Flint arrowheads have been found, as have bronze spearheads and helmets from later times. As well as having at least thirty natural islands, the loch also has the remains of crannogs – artificially built lake dwellings – on its waters. Roman pottery has been found, and the Red Cloaks would certainly have sent probing patrols from the nearby Antonine Wall which linked the Forth estuary and the Clyde. Here, too, the Scotti came from the enclave of Dalriada in Argyll. They originally came from Ireland and met, fought, traded with, and also intermarried with the people of Pictland, and ultimately gave their name to Scotland.

The Strathclyde Britons, whose great fort-capital lay at Dumbarton, controlled much of the loch. A prominent stone in Glen Falloch at the head of the loch is called *Clach nam Breatann*, the 'Stone of the Britons', and is reputed to mark a power boundary. Great families and clans evolved: the

Conic Hill, Balmaha, on the east shore of Loch Lomond, is frequently ascended by visitors and West Highland Way walkers

MacFarlanes, Buchanans, MacGregors, Drummonds, Grahams, the powerful Lennox family and, particularly on the west shore, the Colquhouns who were held in favour by Scottish monarchs. A cattle economy operated on their lands, but by the time of the nineteenth century the old clan pattern had gone and was replaced by landlord and tenant. Modern breeds of sheep came in and many crofting or small farm families left or were 'cleared'. Then came the day of the big estates and larger farm holdings, and in our own day, the growth of Forestry Commission land.

The islands were always effective refuges for key clans and the dead were buried there, often as a part protection against wolves. Saints, too, and church communities used some of the islands as quiet places of retreat. Many island names begin with 'Inch' (from the Gaelic *innis*) which means an island or, sometimes, an enclave of fertile ground. For example, don't say 'Inchcailloch island', because in effect this means Island-Cailloch-Island. Visitors are intrigued by the old saying that on Loch Lomond there are waves without winds, fish without fins and a floating island. A prosaic explanation is that there are waves at the mouth of the burns, eels and water-weed rafts or islets which emerge or re-emerge as the water level rises and falls. The water level does indeed vary – it always did – but nowadays it is controlled to some extent by barrage gates on the River Leven. Loch Lomond water goes to homes and industry in many parts of east and central Scotland, including Edinburgh.

Pleasure craft fill the marina at Balmaha

Cries over the years for a road to be driven up the wooded east side of the loch from Rowardennan to Glen Falloch have – rightly – been ignored. This lovely section of the loch deserves to be left as it is, with its woods and glades, its quiet hillsides and twisting paths. The whole loch is a very rich habitat for a wide variety of fish, plants, trees, birds and animals. A quarter of all known British flowering plants and ferns are to be found, including the rare Loch Lomond dock. The oakwoods are semi-natural and were managed in the eighteenth and nineteenth centuries to provide timber for houses and ships and oak bark for tanning leather. The wood of the alder was used to make clogs and also charcoal, used in the making of gunpowder. Nowadays it is the trees of the Queen Elizabeth forest park that provide timber and there are many picnic spots and walk-trails throughout its shady acres. Shipbuilding and other industries developed in the Vale of Leven and Dumbarton and were linked to the oakwoods. As Glasgow and other communities burgeoned, the by now wealthy merchants built mansions in parkland on the loch shores. In the present day some of these have been developed as hotels, hostels or tourism centres.

The loch contains more species of freshwater fish than any other freshwater loch, including brown trout, sea trout, salmon, perch, pike and an unusual fish called the powan, a kind of freshwater herring which perhaps became landlocked many years ago. It is only found in Loch Lomond and Loch Eck and is protected by wildlife legislation. It is no surprise that Scottish universities have research stations at the loch side.

There is an enormous diversity of wildlife, ranging from hordes of waders and geese – mainly Greenland whitefronts that arrive in autumn in the marshes and mouth of the River Endrick – to the capercaillie, a kind of wild turkey that inhabits woodland, and the all-year ptarmigan (mountain grouse) and golden eagles that frequent the lochside hills. White fallow deer are sometimes seen on the islands, and particularly on Inchcailloch, near Balmaha, and this is a definite link with the past, because white was a sacred colour long ago and could signify good fortune and/or good luck; therefore white beasts, like the famous white hind of the Corrie Ba, in the Blackmount, near Glen Coe, were protected in past centuries. And don't be surprised if you see what looks like a wallaby. Inchconnachan (Colquhoun's Isle), near Luss on the west shore, was once used as a badger retreat by Lady Arran, who also introduced the wallaby and the peccary, a semi-wild pig from South America.

View from Craigie Fort across Loch Lomond

The waters nowadays are happy hunting grounds for cruising and boating, dinghy sailing, canoeing, water-skiing and fishing, and the shores are ideal for walks, cycling, having picnics or, in some corners, horse-riding. There are sites for caravans and tents.

Visitors to the loch mainly come in by two routes: this chapter deals with one of them and with the east shore. The conservation village of Drymen, with its modern gallery and pottery shop and its memories of cattle trysts and the exploits of Rob Roy who collected blackmail there, is the gate to the loch's south-eastern shore. Initially, this is via either the A809 from Bearsden on the fringe of Glasgow or the A811 from Stirling or from Dumbarton; a minor road, the B837, runs from Drymen to Balmaha and Rowardennan, where it ends. Only paths run northwards to Inversnaid. This road can be very busy in summer and it changes in character from Lowland fields to Highland woods and then reaches the loch's islands and hills. There are memories of the Buchanan family – the parish name – and the Drummonds and the Grahams in this corner, and the road also runs past the white houses of Buchanan smithy and the Milton of Buchanan. Soon the steep sides of Conic Hill (from the Gaelic *a-coinneach*, meaning 'mossy') – a marvellous viewpoint for the islands – begin to dominate as the road fringes the loch shore.

The community of Balmaha is then reached, an unforgettable bay of woods, off-shore islands and the large marina that is MacFarlane's boatyard, plus the site of an ancient fort. The West Highland Way path has helped make Balmaha boom and there is now a garden centre, pubs, cafes, hotels, parking space, toilets and a new visitor centre which has audio-visual shows. The nature reserve of Inchcailloch is just across the way, a Mecca for many visitors, and the mailboat run starts from MacFarlane's boatyard. Balmaha is one of the loch's most scenic and much-loved places. This particular corner is a national nature reserve made up of five islands and part of the nearby mainland.

The road here takes a steep twist and rises sharply through a man-made gap. However, it follows an old route which gives this corner its name: the first part, 'Bal', derives from the Gaelic for 'a pass', and the rest is a corruption of a saint's name, 'Machar'. It then pushes north and is often tree-fringed but every now and again an enclave of pleasure for visitors opens up, places such as Milarrochy Bay where parking, picnic spaces, paths and other facilities may be found. As the traveller progresses there are caravan and camping sites and other picnic places and paths, some run by Forest Enterprise as part of the Queen Elizabeth forest park.

The road passes two prominent headlands, Strathcashel Point and Ross Point, and then runs through the heart of the Rowardennan forest. There is a wood carver's workshop at Cashel and a centre run by the Royal Scottish Forestry Society. Both are helping to inspire the regeneration of native woodlands. The remains of early fortified structures lie here, and the name 'Cashel' probably derives from the Latin castellum, although an early Celtic church foundation also stood here. 'Ross' means a wooded headland or point.

Delightful loch and wood scenery follows and the road ends at the little community of Rowardennan, a name associated with St Adamnan, St Columba's biographer. There is a ferry pier, an hotel, chalets, a youth hostel, parking space and toilets and a striking piece of modern sculpture commemorating the opening in 1997 of the Loch Lomond National Memorial Park which is dedicated to those who died in the service of their country in World War II. This eight-mile (13km) section of the loch shore and also Ben Lomond, which forms the Memorial Park, are managed by the National Trust for Scotland (who own much of the ground), Forest Enterprise and the government agency, Scottish Natural Heritage. The memorial sculpture is by artist Doug Cocker. The current plan is to restore the natural woodland.

A ferry runs in season from Rowardennan to Inverbeg, at the mouth of Glen Douglas on the west shore, a route once swum by cattle in the days of the huge droves going south to market, long lines of beasts, the leader led by a boat and the rest following on. Just north of Rowardennan, a huddle of rocks is popularly known as Rob Roy's prison because he is reputed to have held captives there. Rowardennan is also the starting place for most people wanting to climb Ben Lomond, at 3,192ft (974m) the most southerly Munro mountain in Scotland (mountains over 3,000ft [900m] were first catalogued by Sir Hugh T. Munro). It is second only to Ben Nevis for popularity. Much renovation work has had to be carried out on the main path; Ben Nevis gets 85,000 visitors a year and Ben Lomond over 31,000. The National Trust for Scotland have had to ask sponsored walkers to go elsewhere, such is the erosion caused by the pressure of so many boots. The annual Ben Lomond hill

This modern sculpture commemorates the opening in 1997 of the Loch Lomond National Memorial Park dedicated to those who died in the service of their country in World War II

The cross-loch ferry at Rowardennan,
on the east shore of Loch Lomond

race continues, however, with a maximum of 150 participants. The slog to the top takes two to three hours, but the view from the summit is wide and impressive. Note that it is always most important to take heed of the weather forecast and to equip oneself with appropriate clothing.

It is an evocative mountain, commemorated in the old song: 'It was there that we parted in yon shady glen, on the steep, steep sides of Ben Lomond...'

THE ISLANDS ON LOCH LOMOND

THE NUMBER OF ISLANDS ON Loch Lomond depends on a person's definition, because some are tiny and some vanish if the water level rises. The cluster of islands in the southern part of the loch means that this area freezes easily in very cold weather. The two most frequented by visitors are Inchcailloch, close to Balmaha, and Inchmurrin, the most southerly. North of Rowardennan in the narrow, northern section of the loch are the following islands:

ISLAND I VOW, between Inveruglas and Ardlui, and the most northerly islet. The name may derive from Eilean a 'Bho, meaning 'island of the cow', or from the Gaelic for yellow, *buidhe* (pronounced boo-ee). It was a stronghold of the MacFarlanes. This island was visited by Wordsworth.

INVERUGLAS ISLE, close to Inveruglas. The MacFarlanes had a castle on it, but it was destroyed by Cromwell's men.

WALLACE'S ISLE, at the mouth of Inveruglas Water. Sir William Wallace, Guardian of Scotland in the thirteenth century (and the hero of Mel Gibson's film *Braveheart*) may have used it as a guerilla base.

IN THE SOUTH OF THE LOCH

FRAOCH EILEAN, close to Luss. This 'heather island' was reputed to have been used as a prison and a detention centre for nagging women.

INCHLONAIG, between Luss and Strathcashel point. Tradition has it that King Robert the Bruce planted yew trees here to provide bows. This is a Clan Colquhoun island, and was formerly a deer park. It is wooded and hilly.

INCHTAVANNACH, south of Luss: wooded and hilly, with a fine viewpoint hill. There is an ancient monastery situated on it and an expansion centre for St Kessog who died near there in the sixth century.

INCHONNACHAN, meaning 'Colquhoun Island', east of Inchtavannach, separated only by a narrow strait. It has the most attractive wooded bays.

INCHMOAN, south of Inchtavannach and Inchconnachan, with lovely beaches and attractive woodlands. The resident population of fallow deer are frequently seen. It was another Colquhoun controlled island.

INCHCRUIN: in the middle of the loch, east of Inchmoan; it is low and wooded, and separated from Inchmoan by a narrow strait called 'the Geggles'. Mentally ill people once lived there. Its name is obscure.

INCHFAD, also mid-loch, west of Balmaha, and known as 'long island'. It was a former distillery site and is low, wooded, fertile, and recently farmed.

View from Inchcailloch, 'island of women'

INCHCAILLOCH, close to Balmaha, meaning the 'island of women'. It is a part of the National Nature Reserve, managed by Scottish Natural Heritage. It has a nature trail, camping sites and a special barbeque site (by arrangement); it is wooded, with an ancient church settlement and an early convent, home to St. Kentigerna. It is also the burial place for MacGregors and MacFarlanes.

CLAIRINSH, east of Inchcailloch, formerly a Buchanan island. *Clar Innis* is the clan's war slogan.

INCHMURRIN, named after St Mirren. It is the loch's largest island. There is an hotel and a farm, besides other accommodation; it is typified by woodland and is very fertile. Passengers on the mail-boat run often lunch at the hotel. The island is best reached from Arden, on the loch's west shore. There is also the Earl of Lennox's ruined castle where the fugitive King Robert the Bruce was given shelter. Isabella, Countess of Lennox, also took refuge on the island in 1425 after her husband, father and two sons were executed (see Loch Ard, p55). James VI of Scotland (James I of England) hunted deer here. The old chapel is dedicated to St Mirren. In the eighteenth century, women who had 'occasion for temporary retirement' sometimes went there. Part of the island is now a nudist colony.

9 LOCH LOMOND: THE PASS OF BALLOCH AND THE DEVELOPING WEST

THE RAIL TRAVELLER looking down at the northern section of Loch Lomond sees a scene that in several ways has not changed for many years. The railway runs high above the loch and trees hide much of the lower ground of the loch's north-west shore and the busy A82. The length of the loch stretches out below with hardly a sign of a house, the stern face of Ben Lomond dominating all and in the distance the gaggle of islands in the wide southern section can be picked out. The railway comes in from the south and west at Tarbet and gives a far better view of the loch than that enjoyed by car drivers lower down. Queen Victoria called Tarbet 'a small town', which is not strictly accurate for this scattered community, but rightly said it had 'splendid passes, richly wooded, and the highest mountains rising behind'.

Modern boats use the pier at Tarbet, on the west shore of Loch Lomond, close to where the Norsemen once sailed their longships

Modern passengers crossing the isthmus between Loch Long and Loch Lomond get a good view of Ben Lomond: from that aspect it looks pointed and spear-like, rather than the broad-shouldered shape it assumes when seen from further down the loch. It is easy to imagine the Norsemen hauling their longships over from Loch Long and with relief and zest sailing down the loch to the rich pickings on the islands and the more fertile ground. It is easy, too, to think of King Robert the Bruce who took his army across the loch here, a handful of men at a time, some in a tiny boat, others swimming alongside, to gain some rest and respite when their fortunes were low. The king sat reading a romantic story, an act calculated to bolster confidence, while the dangerously slow retreat was made. The great cattle droves came this way and the old drovers' inn at Inverarnan in Glen Falloch has an evocative atmosphere and good views of a lace-like waterfall that pours down the west side of Ben Glas.

The loch's west bank road has been widened and improved in recent years, and one tends to drive up and down it without fully appreciating its attractions. The modern traveller is often on the same line as the eighteenth-century military road, built to tame the clans. The big populations of Glasgow, Dumbarton and the south west mainly reach the loch by way of the A82 and the A81 and the southern town of Balloch (meaning 'a pass' and fittingly named); Balloch draws the key roads together. Those coming from Drymen pass a small hill, Duncryne, called 'the Dumpling' by the locals: it stands on the boundary between Highland and Lowland, overlooking the village of Gartocharn. It is only 465ft (142m) high, but has an impressive view of the loch's islands. Writer and naturalist Tom Weir, the 'grand old man' of the hills and who lives in Gartocharn, says it has the best view of any small hill in the land (see p2–3). It was a fort-site to the people of the past, and they certainly knew what they were doing when they put it there.

Above: This waterfall on the Ben Glas burn near Inverarnan draws eyes from the lower ground
Right: The drovers' inn at Inverarnan, to the north of Loch Lomond, has been welcoming travellers since the seventeenth century

The town of Balloch is *not* scenically attractive. Civic leaders and tourism experts know this and a £60 million visitor centre, which will include a film theatre, shops, information facilities, restaurants and a hotel, is planned for the area, sited at Drumkinnon Bay. The centre, which will also include children's play areas and environmental exhibitions, will be a gateway to the Loch Lomond and Trossachs National Park. Mr Henry McLeish, Minister for Enterprise and Tourism, said the project would be a world-class tourist attraction. In the meantime Balloch is undeniably the gateway to the loch, because it is from Balloch and the mouth of the River Leven that a steady flow of pleasure craft heads out into the loch. Balloch is only 18 miles (29km) by dual carriageway and half-an-hour by train from Glasgow and this corner has shops, hotels, hostels, restaurants, and caravan and chalet sites. Yet within minutes the traveller is surrounded by inspiring scenery, particularly at the memorable Balloch Castle country park and nearby Duck Bay.

The west bank road is flanked in the southern part by the rounded Luss hills and bisected all the way by passes which run through to the glens and great sea lochs of the west which were so strategically important in the past, the old cattle route of the Lairig Arnan, north of Ardlui, Inveruglas and Loch Sloy, Tarbet itself, Inverbeg and Glen Douglas, Luss

The busy River Leven at Balloch, the gateway to Loch Lomond from the south

101

Peaceful Balloch Castle Country Park is only 18 miles by road from Glasgow

village and glen and Glen Fruin which leads to Garelochead, plus the modern B832 to the town of Helensburgh. Travellers pouring into Balloch do not initially see the country park castle or the marina section of the river, but these are well signposted. The country park tells of changing times because the mansion house, built by a private owner in a castellated style, is now open to the general public. It is set in spectacular grounds: 200 acres (81ha) of woodland, parkland and ornamental gardens and it is sited right on the 'bonnie banks'.

The country park was formally designated in 1980 and lies within the 170 square miles (440sq km) of Loch Lomond Regional Park which was created in 1988. The country park is owned by Glasgow City Council and managed by West Dunbartonshire Council. The visitor centre there is managed by the Loch Lomond Park Authority; the latter is made up of a joint committee from West Dunbartonshire, Argyll & Bute and Stirling councils. The park is open all year and is a place for browsing. The staff understand children and many schools and youth groups learn from the knowledgeable Rangers, though this does not mean that they are without a sense of humour: I saw a notice there once which said: 'Unaccompanied children will be sold into slavery'.

Not far from the present mansion there was a thirteenth-century

The wooded islands near Aldochlay and Luss provide secluded havens for boats

Balloch Castle, a power base for the Earls of Lennox before they decided that Inchmurrin was a better stronghold. Lord Darnley, who married Mary Queen of Scots, was the son of the fourth Earl of Lennox; he was murdered in Edinburgh in 1567. The Lennox family held lands and fishing rights at Balloch until the seventeenth century, and then sold these to the Colquhouns of Luss. The old castle has long gone and only the original knoll and a depression which was probably the moat are left. Stones from the castle were incorporated into the 'modern' castle-mansion which was built in 1808 by John Buchanan of Ardoch, one of the original partners of the Glasgow Ship Bank and a Conservative MP.

Successive owners developed the gardens and planted trees and shrubs. In 1915 Glasgow Corporation bought the estate and decided that much of it would be set aside for public use by Glasgow's citizens and thousands of people have revelled in that ever since. The park literature contains a wonderful passage describing its attractions: it was to be 'a place for the tired city mother, and for the joyous laughter and shout of happy childhood; a place for lovers, for Pan and the nymphs of glen and meadow.' It has indeed turned out to be such a place.

A prominent lochside path was originally part of the cattle drovers' route on to the Pass of Balmaha. The north end of the park includes a reputed faery glen.

The visitor centre has an audio-visual show, a fine display of modern stained glass by artist Linda Fraser, a modern mural by Tim Pomeroy, 'touch' material for children, and information about the rich plant life and wildlife of the park, as well as a tea-room and toilets.

Any person driving up and down the A82 in recent years is struck by how visitor facilities have been developed with sensitivity along the west

Balloch Castle was built in the nineteenth century close to the thirteenth-century site of a castle owned by the Earls of Lennox

shore. Good hotels have stood for years at places like Ardlui, Inveruglas, Tarbet, Inverbeg, Luss and Arden, some with their roots in the days of the cattle trade. Now others have been built and older ones renovated and visitor sites include caravan and bunkhouse accommodation, a marina and boat hire at Ardlui, award-winning boat sails at Tarbet, a picnic area and car park on the old road at Firkin Point (ideal for push-chairs or wheel-chair-users), and a caravan/chalet site at Inverbeg which is also the ferry point for Rowardennan.

The old priory ground at Rossdhu House is now an internationally known, up-market golf course. It is easily spotted from the road because the massive, ornamental and heraldic gates of the Colquhouns have recently been renovated and at the time of writing certainly catch the eye. Ross Dhu means 'black-point' and was once the seat of Colquhoun power. Distinguished visitors included Mary Queen of Scots and Sir Walter Scott.

Add galleries at Inverbeg, a viewpoint and sails at Inveruglas and a bagpipe-making centre near Luss, and there are clear signs of tourism vitality.

The battle monument in Glen Fruin has also been renovated. It was there that the MacGregors defeated the Colquhouns in 1603, amid great slaughter and in a bitter power struggle. The Colquhoun widows travelled to Stirling with their dead husbands' bloody shirts on spears and protested to King James VI who took their side. It was one of a series of events which brought retribution on Clan Gregor. They, of course, regarded this protest as a deplorable public relations exercise and carried on in much the same way as before.

Road-side trees tend to blur views of the exquisite archipelago of wooded islands which is why visitors should take to the water, but enough can be seen to demonstrate the beauty of the loch. Both the Wordsworths wrote about two of the islands, although they mixed them up. Keep an eye out for a small statue of a boy set in shallow water: known as Wee Peter and widely rumoured to mark a drowning, it does in fact have a happy story attached to it, having been erected by a man who wanted to commemorate his boyhood holidays.

Ben Lomond and Luss village are the setting for Scottish Television's 'soap' High Road

No visit to the west shore is complete without calling at Luss, the most picturesque of the loch's villages and (as mentioned in the introduction to this book) the site of Scottish Television's series *High Road*, where it is known as Glendarroch. This is the very heart of what was Clan Colquhoun country and Luss is now a conservation village. The name probably derives from the Gaelic *lois*, meaning 'a garden' or 'fertile corner'.

A piper plays tunes at Luss and recalls the days of the clans

Opposite: Luss Kirk stands on a site reaching back to the time of King Robert the Bruce

An older community was known as Clachan Dubh, 'the dark township', possibly because of the nearby hills. A less likely, but attractive story is that centuries ago a Baroness MacAuslin died in France while her husband was fighting there. Her body was brought back home covered in flowers, especially fleur de lus, and this French word for 'a lily' gave the village its name. They allegedly grew to the surface of the grave and local people used them as a charm against illness. A similar story is told in Canada about heather, where the mattresses of Highland soldiers are said to have brought heather seeds from Scotland which took root.

A sign of changing land use can be seen a couple of miles up Glen Luss where a bridge built in 1777 is marked with a tup's (ram's) head. It marks the introduction of 'modern' breeds of sheep, a policy which prompted the 'clearing' of people.

Luss is old. King Robert the Bruce gave John of Luss a charter for the reverence and honour of his patron, St Kessog, and the Luss kirk had a sanctuary area where fugitives were regarded as safe. The graveyard has a Viking burial stone. The present church was built by Sir James Colquhoun as a memorial to his father and five estate staff who were drowned in an accident off Inchtavannach. A mill once stood at Luss and slate was quarried nearby and many of the 'modern' houses were erected by the landowner for the workers.

The annual Luss Highland games, although small in size compared with, say, Braemar, are very popular and the village now includes a loch park centre which has an audio-visual show. The Rangers also organise events and walks at different parts of the loch and keep a polite, but firm eye on boat traffic so that the many different kinds of loch users can co-exist with each other and with the indigenous wildlife.

The writer Tobias Smollet (1721–71) wrote a moving tribute to the loch: 'I have seen the Lago di Garda, Albana, De Vico, Bolsetta and Geneva, and upon my honour, I prefer Loch Lomond to them all, a preference which is certainly owing to the verdant islands that seem to float upon its surface.' However, we'll leave the last word to Sir Walter Scott. Despite his love for Loch Achray and Loch Katrine in the Trossachs, the setting for much of *The Lady of the Lake* poem, he nevertheless called Loch Lomond 'the Queen of Scottish Lakes'.

USEFUL INFORMATION AND PLACES TO VISIT

TOURIST INFORMATION OFFICES

Aberfoyle, Trossachs Discovery Centre, Main Street (April–Oct., and weekends only, Nov-March). Tel: 01877-382352.

Balloch, Balloch Road (April–Oct.). Tel: 01389-753533.

Callander, Rob Roy and Trossachs Visitor Centre, Ancaster Square (March–Dec. and weekends only during January and Feb.) Tel: 01877-330342.

Drymen, Drymen Library, The Square (May–Sept.). Tel: 01360-660068.

Stirling (Argyll, the Isles, Loch Lomond, Stirling and the Trossachs Tourist Board), 41 Dumbarton Road (all year). Tel: 01786-475019.

Tarbet, Main Street (April–Oct.). Tel: 01301-702260.

PLACES TO VISIT

Rob Roy and Trossachs Visitor Centre, Ancaster Square, Callander. Tel: 01877-330342

Scottish Wool Centre, Aberfoyle Tel: 01877-382850

Trossachs Discovery Centre, Aberfoyle Tel: 01877-382352

Queen Elizabeth Forest Park Visitor Centre (David Marshall Lodge), off A821, Duke's Pass, near Aberfoyle Tel: 01877-382258.

Balloch Castle Country Park, Loch Lomond. Tel: 01389-758216

RANGER SERVICE

Loch Lomond Park Authority Ranger Service:
  Balloch Castle Tel: 01389-758216:
  The Park Centre, Luss Tel: 01436-860601
  The Park Centre, Balmaha Tel: 01360-870470
Stirling Council Ranger Service, Tel: 01786-442830
Forest Enterprise Ranger Service, Tel: 01877-382383 or 382258

MAPS

The main walkers' maps for the area include the following OS sheets:

57 (Stirling and the Trossachs area)
56 (Loch Lomond)
51 (Loch Tay)

Also:
Harveys' Trossachs East which covers Aberfoyle and
  Callander north to Balquhidder and Lochearnhead
Harveys' Loch Lomond & Trossachs touring map for cyclists
Others include:
Outdoor Leisure Maps, Sheet 39, Loch Lomond;
OS and Explorer Map, Sheet ll, Trossachs.

THINGS TO DO

* Drive the Trossachs Trail (Callander, Loch Katrine, Aberfoyle, Thornhill and Doune) and travel on the Trossachs Trundler, a bus of yesteryear.
* Cruise on Loch Lomond.
* Sail on steamer up Loch Katrine.
* Walk in the Queen Elizabeth Forest Park.
* Golf, picnic, horse-ride, cycle, sail, canoe, swim, visit historic sites, climb mountains or have gentle strolls, browse, shop, attend Highland games and ceilidhs (informal concerts), eat and drink well and relax.

WALKING SAFELY

When planning a walk there are several important things to do:
* Study the relevant maps carefully and when applicable, seek local advice.
* Give yourself plenty of time: an average walking pace is 3mph (5kph), with half-an-hour to an hour for every 1,000ft (300m) of ascent. Add time for rests – and remember that a walk on a clear, broad path is very different from slogging across undulating and rough moorland of long heather, hidden stones and burns which can rise in spate.
* Check the weather forecast carefully: the weather on the hills can be far more severe than on the lower ground.
* Leave a note with a friend or contact saying where you are going and giving times of setting out and returning.
* Wear stout shoes or boots (the latter are essential for hills and serious walking). Long trousers (rather than shorts) can stop insect or nettle stings.
* Take sensible clothing: it is wiser to strip off in good weather and stick clothing in a rucksack than it is to shiver.
* Take plenty of food and drink, including some extra for emergencies, plus anti-midge and anti-sun lotions.

* If going high or into wild terrain then a map, compass, cagoule with hood, overtrousers and gaiters are normally necessary. A plastic survival bag is wise. In winter add a torch, gloves, a balaclava and extra warm clothing and extra food.
* Inexperienced outdoor people should not go high when ice and snow are on the hills and when an ice-axe and crampons are (or can be) essential. An all-year hillwalker in Scotland is not a rambler, but a mountaineer. Some groups ensure one person has a small first-aid kit.
* Most tourism offices have leaflets on popular and mainly low level walks and Forest Enterprise produces forest map sheets with marked routes. The Ranger service and private agencies conduct guided walks or hire bikes. Details of these can be found in tourism offices.
* Arguments rage over solitary walking. It is a puzzle that lone hillwalkers are criticised and lone yachtsmen are knighted. Solitude can be pleasant, but good sense is needed regarding the weather and the nature of the ground.
* The area covered by this book has magnificent walking, ranging from loch-side strolls to big mountains.
* When on the low ground, do not park your car in places that will make life awkward for local people and particularly not across farm gates or lanes.

COUNTRYSIDE ACCESS

Countryside access in Scotland is a matter of common sense. There is a long-standing Scottish tradition of responsible freedom to roam in appropriate terrain. However, this much cherished folk-right is not a licence to misbehave, nor does it mean people can wander anywhere. It does not mean harming crops, trees or stock, invading house privacy, interrupting reasonable deer stalking patterns, being insensitive to wildlife, or commiting any act of vandalism.

It does mean quietly enjoying a mature freedom, co-existing with those who earn their living on or from the land and being a guardian of the countryside.

The legal position is grey and complex and a matter of the civil and not the criminal law, and lawyers differ in their opinions and beliefs regarding it. A responsible walker seeks to be a friend and ally of the farmer, the forester, the stalker and the rural dweller and should strive to be literate in the ways of the countryside. The three biggest areas of conflict are:

1 Dogs which are out of control and a menace to sheep.
2 The dropping of litter.
3 Carelessness with matches/ cigarettes in forest areas.

The golden rule for any stranger not sure about where to walk is to consult locally. An informal Access Concordat was drawn up over two years ago and covers the high ground. Basically, owners, farmers and outdoor people try to solve problems together. The public's desire to walk, and the needs of those who earn a living on or from the land are recognised mutually (it fell to the writer of this book to receive the Concordat on behalf of outdoor bodies and to speak at the launch). The long-term access pattern will be decided by the devolved Scottish Parliament. However, remember the following golden rules:

* It is a criminal offence to camp or light a fire without a landowner's permission. (An exception can be a mountaineer putting up a tent in a lonely spot and then moving on, leaving no trace, and where tacit consent has operated.)
* Access to some of the Loch Lomond islands can be sensitive because of houses and private jetties and the visitor should check locally.
* Leave all gates as you find them and take all litter home.
* Grouse: The shooting season starts on 12 August and has its peak that month. It ends on 10 December. The shooting butts or shelters are clearly visible and the rule is to stay clear if shooting is going on.

* Stalking: Red deer stags are shot from 1 July to 20 October and hinds from 21 October to 15 February. In practice, the main time is mid-August to around mid-October. Most mountaineers will consult with estates during this peak period as to suitable routes on specific dates, but are not bound legally to do so.
* There are nature reserves and specially protected environmental sites in the area covered by this book. Obey management access requests there.

RECOMMENDED READING

Atkinson, Thomas, *Three Nights in Perthshire* ed. Fergus Wood and Louis Stott (Creag Darach Publications)

Calder, Clair and Lindsay, Lynn, *The Islands of Loch Lomond* (Famedram)

McAllister, Ronald, *The Lure of Loch Lomond: A Journey Round the Islands and Environs* (The Forth Naturalist and Historian)

Stott, Louis, *Enchantment of the Trossachs* (Creag Darach Publications)

—— *Literary Loch Lomond* (Creag Darach Publications)

—— *Ring of Words: Trossachs* (Creag Darach Publications)

PLACE NAMES AND THEIR MEANINGS

Most place names covered in this book are Gaelic (old and modern), others are Brittonic, Scots, modern English or an amalgam of these. Some names have changed over the centuries – spelling was a slapdash affair in the past. Some names of hills and mountains have more than one interpretation: it depended on where you lived long ago. In some cases no one can say with total certainty what a particular name means and can only suggest probabilities.

PLACES

Aberfoyle	Mouth of the muddy pool
Ardlui	High point of the calves
Balloch	A pass or defile
Balmaha	Pass of St Machar
Balquhidder	Several interpretations: possibly 'township in the back country', land of joint occupancy or 'land of the Puidear', a reference to a standing stone. Pronounced bal-whidder
Brig o' Turk	Bridge of the Boar
Callander	Possibly 'hard water'
Duchray	Black sheiling
Gartocharn	House/lands of the place of the cairn
Inverbeg	The little mouth
Inversnaid	Mouth of the Snaid burn. 'Snaid' can mean needle, but a place where woods are opened up has also been suggested
Inveruglas	Mouth of the Black Burn
Kilmahog	Cell of St Chug
Kinlochard	Head of Loch Ard
Lochearnhead	Head of Loch Earn
Menteith	'Mountain' or watershed of the (river) Teith
Port of Menteith	Harbour of (lake of) Menteith
Rowardennan	Point of the height of Adamnan (the biographer of St Columba)
Strath Gartney	Gartney is a man's name
Strathyre	Strath (valley) 'of the corn land'
Tarbet	Boat drag (isthmus)
Trossachs	Possibly 'bristly ground' or transverse glens

LOCHS

Achray	'Of the level field'
Ard	High loch, 'or of the high place'
Arklet	Possibly, 'loch of the snowflakes', a shape of the loch before it was raised and in certain lights
Chon	Of the dogs. Pronounced hon
Dhu	Black
Doine	Deep
Earn	Loch of Ireland (a reference to Celtic missionaries)
Katrine	Theories include a woman's name, 'of the furies', 'place of torment' (linked to legend) or 'of the caterans' (raiders and reivers). Pronounced kat-rin
Lomond	Beacon loch, although shield- or banner-shaped, or 'of the elm wood' have also been suggested
Lubnaig	Of the bend
Venachar	The banks once had marks like cast deer antlers. 'Pointed loch' has also been suggested
Voil	Quick-running flood

MOUNTAINS

A'Chrois	Cross-shaped
Ben A'n	Am Binnean, the Pinnacle
Ben Chabhair	Mountain of the Antler
Ben Each	Mountain of horses. Pronounced ech with the 'ch' as in loch
Ben Ghlas	The grey mountain
Ben Ledi	Mountain of God or light (Beltane) or 'of-the-gentle-slope' or 'full-of-declivities'
Ben Lomond	Beacon mountain (see lochs' list)
Ben Narnain	Obscure. A man's name has been suggested
Ben Tulaichean	The knolly mountain.
Ben Venue	Possibly 'of the caves', or 'of milk' (burns in spate), or 'of the young cattle'
Ben Vorlich (Loch Earn) and Ben Vorlich (Loch Lomond)	Sea bag (bay) mountain in the sense of looking sea-like
Ben a Chroin	'Of the cloven hoof'
Conic Hill	A'Choinneach, meaning 'mossy'
Stuc a Chroin	'Peak of the harm' (bluffs) or 'of the cloven hoof' (a prominent notch)
Stob a Choin	Point of the dog. Pronounced hon

INDEX

Page numbers in *italic* indicate illustrations